What Others Are Saying

Over the past several years Jan Greenwood has worked alongside my wife, Debbie, and helped to lead and pastor the women of Gateway Church. During that time, she has consistently shown herself to be a woman of godly integrity and character. In this book Jan deals with negative misperceptions about relationships between women and presents powerful truths about how women can tear down dividing walls and have healthy relationships with each other. Jesus said that the world will know us by our love for one another, and if you catch the principles that Jan outlines in this book and apply them to your own life, there is no telling what God can do in and through you!

—**Robert Morris**
Senior pastor of Gateway Church
Best-selling author of *The Blessed Life*, *The God I Never Knew*, *The Blessed Church*, and *Truly Free*

Jan Greenwood is one of the finest women I know. I am honored to call her friend. Her dedication to God and her determination to rise above adversity is *so* inspiring. In her very well-written book, *Women at War*, you will be encouraged and strengthened as you fight your own battles. Get a copy today and get one for the girlfriends in your world!

—Holly Wagner
Pastor of Oasis Church, founder of GodChicks
Author of *WarriorChicks* and
A Survival Guide for Young Women

Jan is more than a friend, she is a fighter. Her struggles through life have not stopped her from pursuing the call of God on her life, and I'm honored to be a witness to the wonderful ways she is sharing her story. May her healing, faith, and courage inspire, motivate, and empower you to live the life Christ has called you to.

—Christine Caine
Founder of The A21 Campaign and Propel
Director of Equip and Empower Ministries
Author of *Undaunted* and *Unstoppable*

Few speakers or authors can captivate an audience with their deep knowledge of the Bible and rich personal relationship with Jesus like Jan Greenwood. She doesn't just know about Jesus, she has walked with Him. Her testimony and message ring with clarity and conviction that can only come from a woman who has trusted Him through valley lows and then glorified Him on mountain highs. These pages will challenge everyone who reads them to love Him more wholly, commit to Him more fully, and know Him more deeply. The message and ministry God has entrusted to her will change lives…for eternity.

—**Priscilla Shirer**
New York Times best-selling author
of *The Resolution for Women*

How grateful I am that a woman as wise and deep as Jan Greenwood has tackled the timely subject of how we as Christian women relate to ourselves and to each other. In *Women at War* Jan points us to a better a way—a way of peace, encouragement, and mutual strength for girlfriends everywhere. So honest. So spiritually insightful. So practical. Thank you, Jan, for this amazing gift of help!

—**Kari Jobe Carnes**
Pastor, worship leader, Dove Award winner, and
Grammy-nominated recording artist

Many of the greatest lessons we learn are found in the hardest places. Jan's story was not written on the sidelines but in the midst of the battle. Each page holds within it tested truths and tenacious faith. Her passion for women to embrace all that God has for them is woven within every page. This book will call you to rise and find your place alongside all those with whom we are called to fight—not against, but for!

—**Charlotte Gambill**

Pastor of Life Church, cofounder of "Dare to Be"
Speaker and author of *Now What?*, *Identity*, *In Her Shoes*,
Turnaround God, and *The Miracle in the Middle*

Jan Greenwood unlocks the mysteries of women's relationships throughout the Bible, revealing how God has designed each woman with unique ability, personality, and motivation. When Jan was challenged with a life-threatening disease, she embraced God's love and found inward peace and strength. She brings deliverance to broken hearts and wounded spirits by teaching women to turn from the bitterness of life's battles and to join arm-in-arm with other women as an army of overcomers.

—**Janelle Hail**

Founder and CEO of
the National Breast Cancer Foundation

I just finished reading the first chapter of Jan's book and I have to admit, I wasn't prepared to love it immediately but I did! Relationships are what we all want, and her honest and gracious spirit draws you in and all defenses melt away as she opens up about issues all women face.

—**Karen Evans**

Cofounder and cohost of *Marriage Today*

Jan Greenwood's message tells the story of complete surrender to her Creator in the midst of a battle with cancer and the loss of all that was precious to her as a woman. She lays out a plan to redefine the value of a woman with words such as *wise, influential, beautiful,* and *authentic.*

—Joni Lamb
Cofounder, Daystar Television Network
Executive producer and host, *Joni*
Recording artist and author of *Surrender All*

I have had the great privilege to be up close and personal with this very highly intelligent female leader whose ability cannot be trumped by anyone! Jan Greenwood's successes in business and ministry are not only because of her intelligence, but also because of her sensitivity—to God, her family, and her relationships. Jan has tenderness with strength, and is the best woman I know to address candidly a topic that few women will even admit to. *Women at War* will restore your identity and your femininity in a new and empowering way. It takes the "fight" out of you and puts a "new fight" in you!

—Devi Titus
Vice president of Kingdom Global Ministries
President of Global Pastors' Wives Network

This book is a game changer. I found myself reading with total commitment to a subject that not many will touch, but

Jan Greenwood does with full force and power! This book has so much revelation and gives solutions to everyday battles we as women face. I felt as if I were given a blueprint to discover my purpose as a woman and how to move forward with full confidence in relationships with others. The strategy of God for women is revealed along with tips on how to fight our greatest enemy along the way! Jan has a message that can deliver a cultural shift in thinking for all who will dare to read it! Get ready to see women everywhere live out their God-given destiny!

—**Michelle Brogan**

Pastor, speaker, founder/director of Dance Revolution

Never before in history have women experienced such quality of opportunities and opened doors as we have access to right now. But instead of bringing our nurture and support of one another to bear, too often we fall prey to "feminine fire"—women wounding women. *Women at War* addresses this very present reality, exposing the lies of the enemy and revealing the path to peace. Through her personal experiences of facing pain and learning how to forgive and be forgiven, Jan Greenwood lights the way to restore damaged relationships and develop healthy new ones. As we cultivate feminine strength, celebrate our

God-given purpose, and unite with kindness and grace, women become an unstoppable kingdom force!

—**Wendy K. Walters**
Speaker, consultant, author of *Marketing Your Mind,*
Selling Without Sleaze, and
Intentionality: Live on Purpose!

Jan's story is a beautiful account of God's love for women. She inspires and encourages us to extend natural and spiritual lifelines to one another. In this book Jan captures the essence of God's heart toward His beautiful and precious daughters by bringing revelation of His Word to break strongholds, reclaiming "I am woman," and showing us how to live a life of purpose and destiny.

—**Dorothy Newton**
Speaker, author of *Silent Tears*

Women at War

Women at War

JAN GREENWOOD

GATEWAY
CREATE
PUBLISHING

Most CHARISMA HOUSE BOOK GROUP products are available at special quantity discounts for bulk purchase for sales promotions, premiums, fund-raising, and educational needs. For details, write Charisma House Book Group, 600 Rinehart Road, Lake Mary, Florida 32746, or telephone (407) 333-0600.

WOMEN AT WAR by Jan Greenwood
Published by Gateway Create Publishing
Gateway Create Publishing
700 Blessed Way
Southlake, TX 76092
www.gatewaycreate.com

Cover design by Justin Evans

Visit the author's website at www.jangreenwood.com.

International Standard Book Number: 978-1-62998-591-6
E-book ISBN: 978-1-62998-674-6

First edition

15 16 17 18 — 9 8 7 6 5 4 3 2 1
Printed in the United States of America

Gateway Create gratefully acknowledges the partnership of Charisma House in distributing this book.

Dedication

To my husband, Mark,
And our children, Ashley, John, Luke, and Matthew.
You have granted me a great gift:
The ability to become all God has destined for me—
a helpmate and a mother.
I am forever grateful.

Contents

Acknowledgments

I am so grateful to all the people who helped make *Women at War* a reality. Little did I know the true commitment, encouragement, and resources it would take to birth this book. This project would have been aborted without the support and coaching of so many friends. Thank you seems inadequate for the magnitude of the gifts I have received.

I am grateful to my husband and best friend, Mark. I consider it my paramount privilege and honor to be your wife and the mother of our children. Thanks for your willingness to give me time and grace to love on and share my life with so many others—you are a generous man. Thank you for leading our family to places of greater and greater wholeness and faith. The fruit of this work really belongs to you.

And to our children, Ashley, John, Luke, and Matthew—thanks for the gift of being your mother, for the joy of watching you become amazing men and women, and most of all for your love and grace. You are the greatest joy I have ever known and the most important assignment of my life. After all, I didn't even really know who I was or what my life was about until you came along. Thank goodness you did! I am proud of you.

I'm also grateful to my mom, Marilyn Weston, who all those years ago chose to give me life. Thanks, Mom, for your love and for your patience as you walked this journey with me. I know it cost you a lot. I am blessed beyond measure and I love you dearly. Dad would be proud of the woman you are.

Thank you to Gateway Church, Gateway Create, and the Charisma House publishing team for saying yes. I appreciate your willingness to go above and beyond to help me pour out my heart on paper.

To the women of Gateway Church—I will never be able to thank you enough. You have given me a valuable gift: your trust. You have become family. Thank you for allowing me the privilege of serving with you. There is no other place I'd rather be.

To the women's ministry staff team—I love you with my whole heart. Serving with you is a pleasure. Your friendship is priceless to me. Some days I have to pinch myself as I still find it hard to believe I landed in such a place of grace. You are the finest team a girl could ask for.

This book would not be in your hands without the loyal friendship and amazing mentorship of Debbie Morris—my friend, my boss, and my pastor. She has taught me more about grace and how to love women than any other person. This book is an extension of her vision to help women learn how important it is for us to celebrate one another and cheer each other on.

And, of course, all the appreciation and praise belongs to Jesus for His infinite love for us, His sacrificial grace, and His ever-alive revelation. To Him be all the glory, power, and praise.

—Jan Greenwood

Foreword

Girlfriends. At the risk of sounding like a country western song, many feel you can't live with them and you can't live without them! While girlfriends are vital to the heart of every woman, many of us are shying away because of deep wounds suffered at the hands of someone we called mother, sister, or friend.

As women we instinctively realize we are in a war. But we often wrongly identify our enemy. We often target our own gender as the opponent. We are battle ready when it comes to another female but we are losing the war. Our enemy isn't our friend, sister, or mother; it is Satan.

In *Women at War* Jan Greenwood explores the dark side of wounds inflicted upon us as women by other women and provides hope for a bright future of a godly company of women locking arms in gracious companionship, fighting to change our families, communities, and world.

Jan pulls back the curtain, exposing what we have all experienced at some level along the way. "She said" or "she did" wounds hinder our spiritual growth and destiny. In *Women at War* Jan calls us to take the mountain of healthy relationships and boldly reminds us it can be done!

I have had the privilege of working with Jan for many years. God dropped us in the same office at the same time during a season of transition and, as we formed our relationship, there were plenty of opportunities to not trust or support each other. I still remember the questioning look in her eyes during some tense moments early in our relationship.

I am happy to say that we survived those early days and we still work together—and enjoy a healthy friendship too. The thing is, you can only have healthy friendships if you are healthy. Our relationships are a reflection of who we are. As God tweaked things in Jan's heart that He had been working on for years, our relationship as friends and coworkers became stronger. I watched God continue to heal a very talented woman.

I have had a front-row seat to cheer on my friend as she battled and beat breast cancer, as she faithfully attends to her mom, diligently mothers her four children, loves her husband, and showers women she leads with love and grace. In Women at War, you will find yourself, as I did, loving Jan's vulnerability and bold encouragement to reshape our relationships.

My prayer is that as you read this book, your heart will be open to a new perspective on the women in your life. I pray that God would touch the places of your wounds and give you hope for broken relationships to be restored. I hope that each time you pick up this book, you will be reminded of how important a role you play in declaring a cease-fire on toxic female relationships.

—Debbie Morris
Executive pastor of Gateway Women, Gateway Church
Author of *The Blessed Woman, The Blessed Marriage,*
and *Living Rightside Up*

A Note to Readers

I'm so glad you picked up this book. It's been on my mom's heart for much longer than the two years it has taken her to write it. Perhaps she has always known she has had something to share, something so important she couldn't help but share it.

I have been asked in the past, "What is it like to have such a great mom?" To that I would respond it is rather extraordinary. Not only is she a wonderful wife and mom but she is a leader and an entrepreneur too. She is an example to me in all areas of my life. Because of her, I am blessed to have some of the best girlfriends in the world. She taught me it is OK to be close to girls, and women are one of God's greatest treasures.

Because of her, I know I am not limited by my gender. I am equipped, loved, and called to the destiny God has for me. She is my constant inspiration and my best friend. I am so thankful for the opportunity to share my very special mom with you. I believe she can inspire you in all of the same ways as well.

I want you to know Mom has thought of you every day. You are the surging force that keeps her in constant motion. As she wrote day by day, I saw you right beside her. When life was challenging and it would have been so much easier to give up, she pressed on—because of you. Glean from the lessons she has learned, dive into the stories she so eloquently tells, and hear the message God has so faithfully entrusted to her. She believes in you.

I believe if you let it, this book will transform you. I encourage you to lay your judgments, your weapons, and your wounds at the door. Open up your heart and let it be filled with wisdom. Let the words on these pages speak to the core of your being. You are woman—you matter.

I pray the Holy Spirit would speak tenderly to you and the words that fill these pages would come to life in you.

This is about something much bigger than a book. I believe you could call it a movement.

—Ashley Greenwood

Her children arise and call her blessed.
—Proverbs 31:28

I have a destiny in God. I know the thoughts that the Lord thinks toward me, thoughts of peace and not of evil, to give me a future and a hope.
—Based on Jeremiah 29:11

But then I will win her back once again. I will lead her into the desert and speak tenderly to her there.
—Hosea 2:14

Introduction

A few years ago, I was in a meeting with my coworkers at Gateway Church in Southlake, Texas, trying to come up with a new name for our women's ministry. In just a few short years our church had grown from thirty people who met in our pastor's home to a megachurch of thousands of members and attendees. Our goal was to draw on everything in our experience to come up with a name for our ministry that women of all ages and from numerous walks of life could identify with and would respond to.

The one thing everyone in the meeting agreed on was we wanted to avoid using the word *woman* in the title due to the common perceptions of that word—most of which are not positive.

"It means three kids and a two-car garage."

"It sounds churchy and old."

"Our young ladies won't relate."

"It implies being single isn't OK."

"It's bossy and independent."

"It has too much of the feminist movement attached to it."

"People who've been hurt by women won't want to hang out with them."

We tried numerous substitutes, including sister, chick, even "Gateway Gals." As we sat around the conference table brainstorming how to reach women without using the word *woman*, I began to wonder how all of these connotations came about.

I didn't have such negative views of women as a young child. When I was born my parents were thrilled to have a girl. As I grew up they told me I could do anything and be whatever I put my mind to—and I believed them! According to my mother, when I was in kindergarten, I came out of class one day, hopped in the car, and told her I could run the place without my teacher—I only needed someone to answer the phone, which was too high on the wall for me to reach!

But at some point I discovered in the real world, women don't have perfectly powerful or easy lives. On the contrary, in my attempts to live up to my childhood image of a powerful woman, I was often misunderstood, criticized, and mistreated.

How wonderful would it be if we could change the way women view themselves and one another and, as a result, change the way we are perceived by the world?

As a natural response I withdrew from other women. I came to see them as my enemies, as if we were at war–with one another.

When I had my first child, a daughter, I knew I didn't want to pass that kind of legacy to her. I quickly realized in order to be the best mom I could, I had to gather the courage to explore the painful places in my heart and allow God to have access to them. If I wanted to model for my children the kind of values I longed for them to have, I needed to acknowledge the wounds I'd received, as well as the ones I'd dealt to others, and forgive myself and those who'd hurt me. Then I had to restore damaged relationships and develop some healthy ones.

With my background I wasn't sure it was even possible for me to have positive female friendships. To be honest, I didn't even have much desire to pursue them. But I ached for my daughter to have some.

In the early 1990s, while building a small business with my husband, I served part time as a women's pastor in my local church. There, I discovered I wasn't the only woman who'd suffered significant woman wounds; and not only had I received those wounds, but I began to realize I had given them as well.

During this season, I experienced some major restoration in my life. I also came to realize *healthy female relationships are not only possible—they're powerful!*

In 2006 my family moved to the Dallas/Fort Worth area, and I eventually became a part of the women's leadership team at Gateway Church. Through a divinely orchestrated series of events, I was given the privilege of serving as a pastor to women. My responsibilities include encouraging women to grow spiritually, develop healthy relationships, and learn to encourage one another. As an advocate for them, I am involved in developing our branding philosophies, executing corporate gatherings, participating in leadership development, and serving as a liaison to outside churches. I often get to speak to large groups of women, and I enjoy communicating to them through writing and social media.

As much as I love this amazing position, I consider it my greatest priority to be a good wife to my husband, Mark, and a good mom to our daughter, Ashley, and our three boys: John, Luke, and Matthew. (Yes, we have all four of the Gospels living in our home!) My family has always encouraged me in the pursuit of my God-given calling to come alongside women and help them fulfill their own destinies.

But as I participated in the strategy meeting with my coworkers and pondered my past experiences, I realized most women don't have many—if any—healthy female relationships. Far too often, they talk behind each other's back, engage in gossip, and sabotage their potential friendships. Over time they develop a subtle mistrust of their moms, sisters, girlfriends, female coworkers, and women in general.

The culture we live in confirms their fears by constantly promoting the attitude that women are competitive, slanderous, and malicious. We embrace these lies and end up despising our own gender.

No wonder the word *woman* has such negative connotations!

As the meeting went on, something deep inside me cried out to God for women to be free of these misperceptions. How wonderful would it be if we could change the way women view themselves and one another and, as a result, change the way we are perceived by the world?

If we realize our inherent value, and the importance of female friendships, I believe we can take back our God-given name, with all its rights and privileges. Then the word *woman* can be defined as *wise, influential, beautiful, dynamic, purposeful, visionary, authentic, graceful, dignified, merciful, compassionate, life-giving.*

I've written this book with you in mind. I'm hopeful it

will be more than a case study in female relationships you simply read and set aside. Rather, I wrote it to be an interactive experience. True understanding and transformation happen as we reflect on and process what we are learning. It's enhanced when we discuss it with others.

With this in mind you will see each chapter ends with some questions for reflection. These questions will lead you through a process of self-discovery. If you invest the time to jot down your thoughts, you will consider your own beliefs and experiences in a way that will allow you to partner with God and His Word to experience personal revelation. You won't be dependent upon my opinion or experience, but rather you will be led by the Holy Spirit to greater healing and understanding. I'll walk with you every step of the way. I like to imagine we'd sit down together at my kitchen table, grab a cup of coffee, open our Bibles, and journey together.

Maybe you would consider going a step further and working through this content with a friend or small group. The reflection questions lend themselves easily to a small-group setting, making the job of a facilitator simple. Most of the real spiritual work of my life has been done in the midst of community. We are changed as we share, listen, and gain perspective from those around us. In the end real transformation can be accomplished as we process together.

Although I've added a small amount of space to the reflection questions for you to make notes, I would encourage you to utilize a personal journal for your thoughts. You are about to embark on a journey, one that is worth documenting. I'm going to share with you the things I've learned that have transformed me from a wounded, isolated woman into a staunch supporter of women becoming everything God has called them to be through the power of healthy female relationships. I invite you to take this journey with me and discover for yourself the amazing relationships He has in store for you.

CHAPTER ONE

It's a War

WAKE UP TO THE BATTLE RAGING ALL AROUND YOU

• • •

*For everything there is a season...a time to love and
a time to hate, a time for war and a time for peace.*
Ecclesiastes 3:1, 8, MEV

Patient is not an adjective that usually describes me. That day was no exception. As I sat in a very uncomfortable chair, I shifted my weight from one side to the other. I listened to the steps in the hallway as doctors and nurses passed by. The voices were too muffled for me to hear what they were saying. I sensed someone draw near to the door, but then they passed on by. My heart skipped a beat and my palms sweated.

I distracted myself by focusing on the clicking of the air conditioning unit and the poor choice of paint color on the wall, doing everything I could to divert my mind from the reality of where I was and the possibility of what I might hear in the next few moments. It seemed to take forever.

My thoughts drifted to the words my husband said to me just the week before when I limped into the kitchen. "Jan, if

1

you don't get that taken care of, you won't be able to go to Egypt." He got my attention.

I love to travel, especially on mission trips. Growing up in the Bible belt, it seemed to me like everyone was a Christian and regularly attended church. I hardly knew any unbelievers. I had always heard there were many people in the world who did not know Jesus, but when I started visiting foreign countries, I saw the magnitude of the lost.

In 2009, when I heard about a mission trip to Egypt, I couldn't wait to sign up. Preparing for the trip required a tremendous amount of planning, on top of all my usual life stuff. In the end I focused so much on taking care of everything and everyone else I didn't take very good care of myself.

One day, as I sat at the conference table in my office, I experienced an intense shooting pain in my hip. For a couple of weeks, every time I'd get up or down, my hip hurt. It got better but then got worse again. The pain became so bad I couldn't wear high heels, and I started dragging my leg a little bit.

But I can be hardheaded sometimes. Only at Mark's insistence, and with the threat of missing the trip to Egypt, did I stop and give the matter some attention.

Women have been fighting to be who they are for centuries, especially when they find themselves in situations and circumstances that leave them feeling stripped of their femininity.

I made an appointment with an orthopedist. Two days after seeing him, I went in for an MRI of my hip.

A week later Mark and I returned to get my test results. The doctor opened his computer and showed us the MRI. He pointed at a portion of my hip and explained the tissue was soft and expanding, which was indicative of a possible tumor.

Tumor? My husband and I stared at him, and then at each other, both of us speechless.

The following Monday I went to the hospital for more tests. During a bone scan, the nurse casually asked, "When was the last time you had a mammogram?"

Over the past several years I'd scheduled a mammogram three times; all three times I cancelled the appointment due to my overbooked calendar. (Maybe you can relate. Sometimes I get so busy taking care of others I forget to take care of myself.) Her comment frightened me and tears began to slip down my face. I quietly mumbled something in return, not wanting to let her know how her comment impacted me.

When I finished the scan I was whisked down the hall to radiology for a mammogram and ultrasound. Then I was escorted to that uncomfortable chair in that ugly room I mentioned earlier where I waited alone to see what the consequences would be for overlooking my health.

I AM WOMAN

When I was a teenager, my dad bought me a bright yellow minibike. We lived in the country, where the mailbox was a mile away, the nearest neighbor was down the road and around the corner, and I was more likely to see a cow than a human any day of the week. That little motorcycle gave me freedom to go places and to do things I would never have been able to do without it.

One day as I drove my minibike down the road to visit a friend, wind whipping my hair every which way, I pulled back the throttle and sang at the top of my lungs the Helen Reddy song "I Am Woman."

At this point in my life I had no idea what it meant to be a woman, but I identified with the powerful declarations in those lyrics.

Women often feel the need to declare their femininity. To own it. To fight for it.

I pondered the parallel between that battle and the one I faced in the waiting room that day. Women have been fighting to be who they are for centuries, especially when they find themselves in situations and circumstances that leave them feeling stripped of their femininity.

I snapped out of my memories and back to the moment as I sat in the chair. My heart cried out, *"I am woman! Don't take that away from me!"*

Finally, the radiologist arrived and my fears were realized. "Mrs. Greenwood, you have stage IV breast cancer, and it's metastasized to your hip."

My world spun out of control. I felt weak. Stunned. Shattered.

I knew enough about cancer to understand what I was facing. Cancer would try to steal my femininity, waging an assault on my body, which would threaten the core of who I was. Chemotherapy would sap my strength and expose me to a variety of frightening consequences. It would cause my hair to fall out. Surgical intervention would mean losing one or both of my breasts. My natural strength and zeal for life would be tempered by fatigue and worry. In one fell swoop, I would be bereft of the things that most identified me as a woman. But even more fearful than the effect on my appearance was the very real threat I might die.

I had been attacked—blindsided, really—by a vicious, insidious foe that was trying to take my life as the "spoils of war."

THE GREAT I AM

Within a week of my diagnosis I endured a battery of additional tests and procedures. Two weeks after the diagnosis, I began chemotherapy.

I had become a *patient*.

It became clear my deepest desire would be to leave them a legacy of love.

Not long after my first round of chemo, Mark and I went to a church service. Everyone else stood for worship. I felt so tired and overwhelmed I just sat there.

I closed my eyes, and suddenly it was as if I had entered a room where Jesus was waiting for me.

In my frustration, fatigue, fear, and anger, I confronted Him. "Are You really like this? Are You harsh? Is this some kind of punishment?"

He didn't respond but just kept looking at me with compassion while I vented.

When I finally ran out of steam, I became silent. After a few tense moments I asked the true question on my heart. "Are You going to heal me?"

"I Am," He responded.

I knew what He was saying. Not just "I am going to heal you." He spoke His name to me and revealed His character—the Great I Am. Reminding me who He is, He was saying, "No matter what, Jan, I am enough."

His calm response settled me. Hope began to flicker. In a moment, with my anger and desperation poured out, His peace enveloped me. The weight of His words wrapped around me like a blanket—the Comforter—surrounding my soul. I began to believe God was going to heal me. I knew "I Am" would be with me every step of the way. It was enough.

THE BATTLE FOR WOMANHOOD

I began an intensive year and a half of aggressive treatments—and a lifelong assignment to pursue, apprehend, and maintain my health. After nineteen rounds of chemotherapy, a lumpectomy, and a full round of radiation therapy, God did heal me. I am well.

Coming face-to-face with my mortality changed my perspective and my priorities. Mark and I gave serious consideration to the value we place on family, faith, and friends. I needed to measure my days and carefully consider what my legacy would be.

During the treatment process, I often looked into the faces of my children, feeling the depth of my love for them.

If I could only do a few things before my death, what would I choose? What would my last words be? What treasure would I bestow on them?

It became clear my deepest desire would be to leave them a legacy of love.

I held my children in my arms and told them, "I love you." I asked them to forgive me for the times I'd caused them pain. I talked about the faithfulness of our God and assured them of His willingness to heal all our hurts—physical, emotional, and spiritual.

But I decided I wouldn't stop there. I would start a revolution of love that would go beyond my own children and reach women everywhere. For years the Lord had been teaching me about the battle raging for our femininity and our relationships. He had been speaking to me about the power of love to restore them. I wanted to share what I'd learned while exposing the threats, lies, and wounds women impose on one another—first for the benefit of my daughter, Ashley…and then for my future daughters-in-law…and finally for all the women I love, even for those I didn't personally know.

WINNING THE WAR

I wish I could tell you I was spared the ravages of my war against cancer or give you a story of instant healing without suffering. The truth is. I experienced grueling negative side effects from my chemotherapy treatment. My hair fell out, challenging my self-esteem. I had to surrender the diseased portion of my breast to surgery and faced terrible battles with fear. I walked with a painful limp for a long time, and it has taken me years to regain my physical strength. I didn't get to make the trip to Egypt that was so important to me, and I tasted the disappointment of lost opportunity.

But I have won some major battles along the way. In the process of walking through this frightening season, I overcame not only cancer but also many of my fears, wounds, and insecurities. I found the courage to fight for my womanhood on both the natural and the supernatural fields. I discovered I am eternally secure in the hands of a loving, warring Savior who proves His faithfulness to me over and over. I have retained my femininity and embraced its power. I now know who I am is only superficially related to my physical appearance.

Now when I hear or say, "I am," it gives me a boost of strength as I recall God's message to me of His love and power. Every day I remind myself, "I am well. I am woman."

The same God who championed me through my struggle with cancer can bring about victory in the war for our femininity as well. I now know no disease, weapon, or wound can steal who we are. Our enemy is strong, but this battle does not have to overwhelm us. Let me assure you, we are on the winning side. When women come together, united in love, we are powerful.

• • •

QUESTIONS FOR REFLECTION

Maybe you've been in a battle similar to mine. Maybe it hasn't been a fight for your health, but rather a fight for your family or your values or your faith. I'd like you to consider your own story as you begin these first moments of reflection. Think about your journey—where you began and how far you've come. From this position we will begin to dig a little deeper into your perspective on your gender and the female relationships all around you. Now is a good time to open your journal and begin to record your experiences and thoughts.

What does "femininity" mean to you? What does it mean to be a woman?

Describe one or two of the most important female relationships in your life. Are/Were these positive or negative experiences? Why?

Describe a moment or a season when you began to realize there was a war among women. What was happening in your life?

How did you respond to those circumstances? How did you respond to God in those circumstances? Take a minute to process this moment or this season with God.

Let's pause here and ask God some questions. Maybe this is a new way of communicating with God. He loves to speak to His daughters to tell us the truth about how He sees us and loves us. Just stop for a moment and get quiet. Don't be afraid; He's a good God. He's gentle and kind, and He loves you very much. He speaks in thoughts or in pictures, and sometimes in just an impression. Listen.

God, what lies have I believed about me as a woman?

What lies have I believed about my femininity?

What is the truth about me? About my femininity?

Write down what you hear. (This would be a great moment to make your first entry in your journal.) If it makes you feel yucky or ashamed, it's not God. On the other hand, if it makes you feel loved and valued, it most assuredly is God!

Take what He said about you and your femininity and declare it! Write it down or even share it. Boldly declare the truth of what God says about who you are!

CHAPTER TWO

Propaganda

KNOW YOUR TRUE ENEMY AND HIS LIES

• • •

*Finally, brothers, whatever things are true, what-
ever things are honest, whatever things are just, whatever things are pure, whatever things are lovely, whatever
things are of good report, if there is any virtue, and
if there is any praise, think on these things.*
Philippians 4:8, MEV

Propaganda is a deceptive and prolific weapon of war because every conflict is fought on two battlegrounds: the battlefield itself and in the minds of the people engaged in conflict. We must remember whatever is communicated from our enemy's perspective will be laced in propaganda. Our enemy, Satan, is a liar. His mission is to kill, steal, and destroy. He is skilled at misleading people with distortions, exaggerations, subjectivity, inaccuracy, and even out-and-out fabrications. Our modern day submersion in all kinds of media is often the perfect place for him to spread his campaign of lies—especially about women.

Today's media is one of the most challenging and pervasive methods of war being used in the assault on women. Television, movies, and music shape our perception of what is normal, what is acceptable, and what should be sought after. What we see and hear influences us, whether or not we are aware of its impact.

Over the years the media has become progressively negative about women—and progressively more influential. Women in general are portrayed as mean, manipulative, selfish, or stupid.

Even movies that are for children have exploited the ugly side of female relationships. Cinderella had a wicked stepmother and two hateful stepsisters. Snow White was betrayed and almost murdered by a jealous woman who despised her for her beauty. Ariel spent all her time longing to be something other than the mermaid she was and working hard to forfeit her royal position for an emotional fantasy, even if it meant defying her father and neglecting the needs of her sisters and her commitments to the community. The more recent Disney princess movie *Brave* has a plot focused on the strife between a mother and a daughter, with the implication that a daughter must rebel in order to find her own way. These stereotypes are subtle and prolific, but they aren't just focused at our youngest ladies.

In the battle of life we must remember whatever is said on the enemy's side is propaganda. He is a liar.

The launch of daytime soap operas in the 1960s began to slowly erode the value and beauty of women. Day after day viewers lived vicariously through the dramatic stories of people who only appeared to live in reality. As our mothers and grandmothers watched daytime TV, their sense of what was normal, healthy, and appropriate in relationships was altered.

Today, you and I have seen the launch of several TV programs that include the term *housewives*. These shows have taken the relationships of women to a whole new level of ugliness. Every episode is a verbal barrage of cursing, backbiting, and injury. We get a weekly onslaught of treachery, verbal abuse, slander, plotting, and pain. Everything in the series confirms our worst fears and cultural lies. The women portrayed in these shows are in pain and lack any real solutions for their struggles. Although we instinctively know what we are watching is wrong, we can't seem to tear ourselves away. Week after week, we are steeping ourselves in this cultural influence, confirming this is how "real" women treat one another.

And we call these things "entertainment."

These and many other reality shows, books, movies, and music are filling our airwaves with negative press about women—and impacting both our daughters and us. They imply women are a strange mix of friend and enemy who relate to one another through catfights and competitions, leaving girls to wonder if the only way to be seen and heard is to follow this insane model.

This is not what God had in mind when He created women.

GOD'S REALITY

In order to understand how God views women, we need to go all the way back to the beginning, to the Garden of Eden.

Adam was created by God from dirt, shaped and formed by His hand. When God breathed His own breath into Adam's body, he lived. Adam was unique: the only thing in the garden created in God's image. He was perfect.

God gave Adam a tremendous assignment: to name all the animals He had created. As he chose a name for each one, Adam demonstrated the same vivid imagination as his Father. We don't know how long it took Adam to complete this task or how many creatures came before him, but we know in the end Adam realized there was nothing in the garden like himself. There was no other creature crafted in the image of God.

When Adam became aware he was different, God moved in with a final creative miracle. He divinely sedated him and performed the first surgical procedure. He reached into Adam's side and removed a portion of his rib bone. While Adam slept, God created a mate for him, literally from his flesh and blood.

Why would God use a bone from Adam's body to create his mate?

Let's think for a moment about the purpose and power of our bones. They not only provide skeletal support for our bodies, but they actually produce life. Scripture tells us life is in the blood (Gen. 9:4; Lev. 17:14; Deut. 12:23). The marrow, the soft part of the tissue inside our bones, is a factory of blood production, constantly developing the resource that supplies the body with oxygen, nutrients, and a defense system.

God took this living, life-giving portion of Adam and used it to create another human.

When Adam awoke, he saw this one final miracle. Then he did what he'd been doing for a long time. He named her. He called her woman, saying, "This…is bone of my bones and flesh of my flesh" (Gen. 2:23, ESV). The Hebrew word for woman literally means *out of man*.

Like Adam, she was remarkable. Unique. Made in the image of God. She was the perfect partner for him. But there was also something else special about Eve.

Adam needed a miraculous procedure to produce another life. He had life in him—bone and blood—but it would sustain only his own body. Eve also had the ability to sustain life within her own body (bone and blood), but more than that, she was formed with a womb.

The first woman was fashioned to carry life in her womb. She would be a life-giver and a life-sustainer. She would partner with Adam to produce children in a setting of complete safety and intimacy. Together, the man and woman would build the first family.

Satan hates you. He hates all mankind, but he especially despises women.

In the garden Adam and Eve walked and talked freely with God, continually communing with Him. This is how God intended life to be for all of us. No sin, no heartache, no pain, no sickness, not even arduous labor. They could do anything, have anything, and eat anything with just one exception. As long as they refrained from eating the fruit of the one designated tree in the middle of the garden, everything else was theirs to enjoy.

But things didn't quite work out as you would expect. Our enemy, Satan, also had access to the garden. He used a beautiful, talking serpent—one of the creatures Adam had named—to lure the woman into sin. He drew near to her as a companion in the garden and sought out an opportunity to talk with her about what God had said to her and Adam. He filled her mind with propaganda by asking her a question or two about the one thing God had told them not to do: eat fruit from the forbidden tree. He went even further by slandering God's character, implying He was a liar. The serpent used subtle implications to lead the woman to reason if she ate from the tree of the knowledge of good and evil she would be like God.

This is how powerful propaganda can be. She and Adam were already like God. They were created in the image of God. She already possessed the thing she was convinced she lacked. Satan was cunning, laying a foundation of doubt in her mind. In the end the woman used her free will and ate the fruit, then shared it with Adam.

Immediately their reality changed. They knew they were naked and now they were suddenly ashamed. When they heard God coming, their guilt drove them to run and hide. For the first time ever, they experienced fear.

When God inquired about their fruit-eating escapade, they blamed one another.

God is not a liar and as promised there were terrible consequences for all involved—the man, the woman, the earth, and the serpent. Interestingly, He began with the serpent.

Genesis 3:14–15 says God told the serpent: "Because you've done this, you're cursed, cursed beyond all cattle and wild animals, cursed to slink on your belly and eat dirt all your life. I'm declaring war [some versions say enmity, which is the strongest word for hate] between you and the Woman, between your offspring and hers. He'll wound your head, you'll wound his heel" (THE MESSAGE).

In a moment the war was launched between Satan and the woman.

There were also big consequences for the first couple. He was destined for a life of toil and she to giving birth in pain. The woman, created to sustain life and to birth love, instead gave birth to hate and death. It was a catastrophic moment for mankind.

To protect them from making the same mistake again, God removed Adam and Eve from Eden specifically so they would not have access to another tree in the garden, the tree of life. Being so dramatically evicted must have devastated their souls even further.

Yet in the midst of their fear, guilt, and shame, Adam declares a portion of Eve's divine purpose by giving her another name, Eve, meaning "mother of all living."

OUR MORTAL ENEMY

Can I let you in on a little secret? Satan hates you. He hates all mankind, but he especially despises women. Satan knows Eve heard the curse spoken over him, and he realizes her offspring can crush his head. Therefore, he is terrified of you, and he will do anything to kill your ability to produce and sustain life. You make him shake in his boots because you are a serious threat to his plans.

This is why we are in this very real war.

This is why the enemy is continually striving to stir up war between you and your children and between you and other women. He wants to pepper your mind with lies and wound you through the words and actions of others so he can deceive you and reduce your capacity to overcome him.

When we pit ourselves against each other, we perpetuate the hatred birthed in the garden. He gets excited when we tear one another down, because he relishes the opportunity to bruise our heel. He wants us to become haters and life-destroyers instead of lovers and life-givers.

Unfortunately I'm a lot like Eve. Far too often I listen to the implications of the enemy, entertain his lies, and reason myself into sin. Why?

For years, my family has watched *Survivor*, the first "reality" TV show. We have been fascinated by the power of people to persevere toward a goal through incredible hardship. We've also been amazed by the depth of treachery, deceit, and disrespect one human will show to another, often for no clear reason. The producers put normal people in a pressure-cooker situation, manipulate the circumstances to create maximum stress, and then stand back to watch the fireworks.

This is not so different from Satan's strategy.

We live in our very own false-reality show filled with propaganda. There is a producer (Satan) and a team of directors (demons) who work overtime to add pressure and conflict to the everyday realities and stresses of being human. They plot against our natural strengths and needs to create one challenge after another, where some small comfort or hope, which seems so essential, is offered as the grand prize. We play blindly, buying into every lie, experiencing short-term victory but long-term rejection. We strike out at others (especially women) while injuring ourselves. We fail to experience intimate, interpersonal relationships the way they were meant to be and instead attack those who have the potential to love us, build us up, encourage us, and bring us closer to the one who created us.

As we watch the world around us and listen to the lies of the enemy, instead of evaluating the messages, we receive them into our spirits, ponder them, talk about them, and even own them. These negative perspectives eventually form our opinions, ideas, and even our belief systems. As we are deceived, we become our own worst enemy.

LABELS

A label is used to identify something, to tell us what it is and who it belongs to. Our enemy uses labels as a weapon to brainwash our thinking and create doubt about what God has said to us, giving us derogatory perceptions of who we are and who God is.

From an early age, we tend to accept the opinions of those around us. If friends, teachers, family members, or even strangers point out our mistakes and highlight our weaknesses, we experience shame, fear, and disappointment. By the time we reach adulthood we are scarred with all kinds of negative thoughts and connotations about ourselves.

Have you ever thought any of the following words

described you? (Go ahead, put a checkmark next to any that seem to fit your past or current self-perception. And write in any negative adjectives that aren't on the list.)

- Fat/overweight
- Lazy
- Worthless
- Incompetent
- Stupid
- Foolish
- Unwanted
- Bad
- Ugly
- Stubborn
- Clumsy
- Irresponsible
- Unreliable/ undependable
- Unstable

God never labels us, but He loves to name us.

The enemy constantly whispers to our hearts that such labels apply to us, and because we live in a false-reality world, we believe him. Our private insecurities are confirmed when other people put those labels on us. Soon we believe a whole host of lies.

Satan wants us to believe these labels define who we are. He rejoices when we see ourselves according to these false perceptions. If he can convince us we are defined by our shortcomings and failures, or God's Word is not trustworthy, he can stop us from being who we really are. These labels, and the painful experiences associated with them, are the instruments he uses to *bruise our heel*.

NAMES

God never labels us, but He loves to name us. Adam gave Eve two primary names: "woman" and "mother of all living." Those names still apply to you and me. God calls us "women" and "mothers." We carry Eve's DNA within us.

The name "woman" is foundational, prophetic, and powerful. It speaks to us and to others about our real identity and our real purpose. We were given this name as a gift. Somewhere along the way, we handed it over to our archenemy and allowed him to attach all kinds of ugly labels to it.

God loves women so much that He is speaking even more powerful and prophetic names over us today. Some of these names were never spoken over our grandmothers or even our mothers. I believe there are more names to come for our daughters.

There is only one sure way to overcome the lies of the enemy, and that is to know the truth.

Here are some of the names God is speaking over women today. Which of the following resonate with you?

- Rescuer
- Ambassador
- Revolutionary
- Abolitionist
- Judge
- Defender
- Executive
- Governor
- General
- Representative
- Friend
- Neighbor

- Advocate
- First responder
- Leader
- Missionary
- Warrior

There is only one sure way to overcome the lies of the enemy, and that is to know the truth. You and I have the ability to reject the labels and lies of our enemy so we can embrace and recover our God-given names. If you have been listening to a crafty serpent about what you lack or allowing him to interpret what God said, take a moment to repent and apply the remedy of truth. Remind yourself that you are the daughter of God and you have everything you need to be a life-giver.

AN ORIGINAL DESIGN

No matter what new names God may be speaking over us today, we must not forfeit His original names for us. From the beginning, you and I were uniquely designed to conceive, carry, bring forth, and nurture life. We can bring beauty, hope, and comfort into situations and circumstances. We can speak life where there is death, hope where there is hopelessness. And regardless of how many biological children we have (or even if we don't have any), we can bear an endless number of spiritual children.

I want my daughter to embrace her God-given name and believe her gender is a blessing and not a curse. I want you to believe it too.

Over the centuries our enemy and our culture have struck malicious blows against our gender by teaching us women are deadly. We've forgotten our true purpose and ability and allowed our fears and misperceptions to reason us into agreement with Satan. As a result, we turn against each other and our own children—both biological and spiritual. We kill the fruit of our womb. We reject the strength of our name. We perpetuate the lies of our enemy, and we sustain the war among ourselves.

This is the cultural standard of femininity in our day. This is the hype our daughters and we contend with on a daily basis.

In the past I have believed some lies and labels that caused me to behave as if I was ashamed of the name *woman*. But no more. I cannot stand by any longer and quietly allow the culture I live in to place shame on me or on the women around me. I want my daughter to embrace her God-given name and believe her gender is a blessing and not a curse. I want you to believe it too.

• • •

QUESTIONS FOR REFLECTION

I wonder what you think about the war I have just laid before you. Many women tell me they knew there was more going on in their female relationships, but they didn't know how to express it or understand it. It's like we are familiar with the grind of conflict, yet we are blinded by the propaganda and our own desires. As we begin to sort through your experiences, take some time to thank God for the privilege of being a life-giver. The more we embrace our identity, the greater will be our freedom and our impact. Grab your journal and let's get started.

In what ways have you allowed our culture to shape your opinions of women? What about your opinion of yourself?

What labels have you allowed the enemy to apply to you? What have you believed about yourself as a woman? Do those labels you identified agree with God's opinion of you?

Take some time to talk with God about His opinion of you. Reread the list of true, God-given names listed in this chapter. Which ones stand out to you? Which ones resonate with your heart? Ask God to highlight the ones He wants to speak to you. Allow Him to declare those names over you—and maybe some that aren't on the list!

"So God created human beings in his own image. In the image of God he created them; male and female he created them" (Gen. 1:27). In Genesis 3 the enemy not only stole Eve's place in the garden, he also tried to steal the image of God from her. But God's original plan for her—and for you and me—is that we would be His image-bearers on the earth. Read the following scriptures about some of the characteristics of God.

- God is holy (Ps. 77:13, Rom. 12:1)

- God is righteous (Matt. 6:33, Ps. 51:14)

- God is powerful (Ps. 62:11)

- God is beautiful (Ps. 27:4)

Now spend some time and ask Him to reveal how you are like Him in those areas. You are made in His image! (This is a great place to journal your discoveries!)

> Over the centuries, our enemy and our culture have struck malicious blows against our gender by teaching us women are deadly. We've forgotten our true purpose and ability and allowed our fears and misperceptions to reason us into agreement with Satan.

Consider this statement in light of the following passage:

> God blessed them and said to them, "Be fruitful and multiply, and replenish the earth and subdue it. Rule over the fish of the sea and over the birds of the air and over every living thing that moves on the earth."
> —Genesis 1:28, MEV

What is God's true purpose for women?

CHAPTER THREE

The Ravages of Engagement

WOMEN FIGHTING WOMEN LEADS TO DEATH

• • •

He gives the barren woman a dwelling, making her
*the joyful mother of children. Praise the L*ORD*!*
Psalm 113:9, MEV

War puts everyone at risk. Although we may show incredible strength and resilience in battle, conflict exposes us to a host of risks and consequences. Some of the most obvious ones are death, injury, displacement, and separation of families. In addition to these threats to individuals, society as a whole suffers a general destitution that leaves many with no choice but to fend for themselves. I can't think of many things more traumatizing than being caught up in a hostile environment day after day, desperate to protect myself from the consequences of war.

This is true not just in an armed conflict, but also in the battle for our gender. Given our vulnerability to the lies of the enemy, you and I must become aware of the engagement raging around us so we can protect ourselves and those who are most vulnerable: our children.

Many of us suffer significant emotional pain as a result of how other women have treated us. And if we're honest, we've been rather nasty ourselves on occasion. We've reacted out of our own vulnerable places, lashing out at one another. What we end up with is a general lack of trust of other women—even those we should be closest to: mothers, sisters, girlfriends, etc. We grow up despising our gender, wounding one another with our unrealistic expectations, and isolating ourselves from meaningful female relationships.

Let's look at some of the underlying issues that contribute to this problem so we can discover what we can do about it.

As I see it, there are two primary reasons women war against one another:

1. Satan hates us. Because there is continual war between the enemy and us, he constantly sets in motion opportunities for us to doubt the heart of another toward us. If we don't know the truth about who we are and what we are called to, we will fall victim to his plots.

2. We've consistently wounded one another. Sometimes in the heat of the battle, you can become confused about who's the enemy and who's your ally. Thinking you are defending your own territory and righteously assaulting what is evil, you strike out at those who are

on your team. Not only that, but those who should be for us are often busy delivering their own painful wounds. The longer you fight against your own clan, the more intense the battle and the more clouded your thinking. We know there is a war, but we have been misled about who *really* is our enemy.

My friend Amy had an experience with a woman who had been wounded by the battle for femininity. She was on a bus headed to a retreat, and felt a little nervous because she'd never done anything like this. She didn't know the other participants and wasn't sure what to expect.

Many of us suffer significant emotional pain as a result of how other women have treated us.

As the trip got under way she tapped the shoulder of a beautiful woman near her and asked, "When's lunch?" The woman snapped back with a rude response, not even bothering to make eye contact. "That was mean," Amy thought. "What's her problem?"

On the surface this young woman looked like she had it all together. But as the weekend progressed, she shared her story. Amy discovered she had gone through more heartache in the past few years than anyone should experience in a lifetime. Her own heart began to soften. Amy felt so much compassion for her, tears streamed down her face. She couldn't imagine suffering such pain. Eventually, Amy gathered her courage and dared to approach the woman again. By the end of the retreat, they had overcome their rough start and begun to form a friendship.

When you encounter someone who swings a painful sword your way or gives off a vibe of meanness, look past the surface and realize something is going on in her heart. If she doesn't seem to have the ability, desire, or willingness to connect with other women, it's likely she is experiencing the ravages of war.

WOMEN WOUNDS

Have you ever been forced into a situation that was out of your control? Have you ever done someone a favor and had him or her despise you for it? Have you ever been abused at the hands of a barren and bitter woman?

Scripture tells us about lots of women who acted ugly. One of the saddest stories involves two wounded women who repeatedly took out their pain on each other.

For years Sarah listened to her husband, Abraham, tell about a miraculous encounter with God during which He promised Abraham would have a son and become a father of nations, with numerous descendants. Although Sarah was beautiful, wealthy, and loved by her husband, she was barren. Sarah could not bear children in her physical body.

We know there is a war, but we have been misled about who *really* is our enemy.

The word barren is so harsh. When we are barren, physically, emotionally, or spiritually, we struggle with a barrage of negative emotions. Often we will feel not only sad or angry, but also inadequate. We interpret our inability to conceive as a character flaw, or worse, a consequence of sin. We blame ourselves and possibly even conclude that we have failed those we love. We might even think God doesn't want us to be a mother, or a life-giver in any sense.

These are all lies.

It is God's desire that you and I be life-givers, physically and spiritually. I don't understand why God's will doesn't always come to pass in the natural during our lifetime, but I'm not confused about His heart. God would not have placed wombs in our bodies if He did not desire for those wombs to give life.

God has unlimited grace and hope for those who find themselves in this situation. There is an amazing promise to barren women found in Isaiah 54:1–3 (NIV):

> "Sing, barren woman, you who never bore a child; burst into song, shout for joy, you who were never in labor; because more are the children of the desolate woman than of her who has a husband," says the LORD. "Enlarge the place of your tent, stretch your tent curtains wide, do not hold back; lengthen your cords, strengthen your stakes. For you will spread out to the right and to the left; your descendants will dispossess nations and settle in their desolate cities."

In this passage God makes a significant promise. He says in the places where we are barren, He will bring forth spiritual children. Even if your natural womb is not functioning properly, that doesn't mean you can't be what God has called you to be. As a matter of fact a woman who is physically barren often feels the call to be a mother more passionately than the woman with a child in her arms. You see, often in our place of lack there is deep desire. Your desire is amplified and empowered because it reflects a God-given capacity meant to produce fruit.

Most of us could identify someone who has struggled with the pain of infertility. But if we could see one another's spiritual wombs, I think we would be shocked. Many women are walking around with their wombs dormant and empty. This need not be the case. Our spiritual wombs are not hampered by our age, monthly cycles, or disease. They are always open and ready to receive what God is ready to impart.

The fruit of our spiritual wombs is so powerful it can take back desolate places and even restore entire families. If we make the choice to rejoice, even in our pain, and then stretch beyond our limitations, we will see descendants everywhere.

SARAH

As Sarah faced her barrenness and aged far beyond her childbearing years, she found it more and more difficult to believe Abraham's promise of numerous children could possibly apply to her. Concluding God must have some other mother in mind, she turned to the common cultural practice of her day and offered her maid, Hagar, as a surrogate mother.

Sarah gave up on waiting to see if the call God had placed on Abraham would include her and willingly abdicated her position. More than that, she forced another woman to fulfill a promise that was meant for Sarah.

As Hagar's belly grew, so did Sarah's insecurity. She began to war with Hagar. Sarah went to Abraham and demanded he do something about the slave. But he had no idea how to resolve a fight between these two women. Out of deep bitterness, jealousy, and grief, Sarah took out her pain and frustration on Hagar, abusing her harshly. Apparently Hagar returned the favor, despising Sarah.

Even if your natural womb is not functioning properly, it doesn't mean you can't be what God has called you to be.

The hate between these two women became so intense Hagar saw no choice but to run away. Pregnant and reviled, she left her community, her family, and her home and went into the desert, where she faced endless miles of wilderness and almost certain death.

God met Hagar in the desert and spoke comfort and hope to her. He also instructed her to return to Abraham and Sarah. The encounter in the wilderness must have been profound since Hagar obeyed, despite the fact that there was no real change in her circumstance. Later, when she bore a son to Abraham, as her mistress had instructed, Sarah rejected both Ishmael and his mother.

This story grieves me in many ways. I hate that women are sometimes barren. I hate that we are often so desperate to bring about a prophetic promise we take the situation into our own hands. I hate that we draft other people into service for our own agendas. I hate that women war against their gender and grow to despise one another.

PROGRESSION OF PAIN

Many of us are trapped in the aftereffects of war. We've experienced such horrific wounds and seen such massive damage in relationships we suffer from a form of post-traumatic stress disorder. There is a flat, detached tone to our lives. We struggle with a number of hard-to-define consequences like depression, anxiety, fear, and restlessness. We can easily be set off by situations that are similar to our past battlefield experiences. We may recover from our outer wounds, but the damage done in our souls continues to haunt us.

Many of us are trapped in the aftereffects of war. We've experienced such horrific wounds and seen such massive damage in relationships we suffer from a form of post-traumatic stress disorder.

No matter the source of our battle scars they have a profound effect on our lives. They create places of lack in our souls. If our wounds remain unhealed we will experience a progression of pain that will leave us with an inability to receive and give love.

Here is how I see this progression of pain happening for women:

1. We experience a form of emotional deadness (barrenness). We lose our ability to nurture others, sometimes even our own children, because we have not been nurtured ourselves. Our pain is so intense we lose our long-term perspective. We focus only on what we can do to alleviate our suffering.

   The problem is that if we refuse to feel pain, we will also be unable to feel joy. Our natural emotions become flat, because neither extreme is allowed.

   I believe this condition is directly related to the massive rise of abortion in our generation. We as a culture don't esteem the value and potential of a woman's life-giving power or of our offspring. Instead we consider our babies to be a curse, and we prioritize the relief of our pain and the convenience of our own needs and concerns over protecting their destiny. When we extinguish our life-giving capacity, our spiritual wombs become dormant. Cooperating with the plans of the enemy, we take matters into our own hands, casting off life, new relationships, and fresh dreams before they have an opportunity to grow.

2. If our wounds remain unhealed, insecurity grows. We see ourselves, and others, from an improper perspective. Lacking love, we become rude, fearful, and prone to slander.

Since we don't want to be rejected, we isolate ourselves from the perceived threat: other women. We become autonomous and independent, thinking we don't *need* anyone. Often we embrace men in an improper manner, using our sex appeal as a way to connect. This approach to men confirms the attitude women are not to be trusted but rather treated as objects to be used. As a side effect, sexual abuse and harassment are tolerated.

3. Now our inherent ability to nurture becomes misdirected. Since we think we can depend only on ourselves, opening up to another person for help or love, especially a woman, seems frightening and risky. This kind of vulnerability is contrary to the coping tools we've developed. In an attempt to fill the void in our hearts, we smother our children and mother our men. Our kids feel suffocated rather than loved, becoming either weak and underdeveloped or rebellious and demanding of their independence. A husband will reject being mothered, either becoming passive in the relationship or acting out in some way to demand the respect he needs. Since we don't know how to properly lead our families with grace, we resort to control and manipulation.

4. The final result is a long string of broken relationships with both men and women. We lack

the emotional health and relational skills to overcome the bumps. It seems easier to quit and move on than to restore damaged relationships. Often we will go so far as to reject the strengths of our gender and become masculine in our thinking and approach to life. We close off a portion of ourselves that is tender and nurturing. Out of our wounding and disconnection, some women go so far as to completely reject their femininity, entertaining a lifestyle of homosexuality. Some simply shut down all emotion, becoming robotic and flat, finding themselves unable to intimately connect with others.

To overcome this pattern of pain, you and I have to lay down our carnal weapons of fear, self-defense, and hate, and pick up some righteous weapons that are effective for overcoming the lies and wounds of our true enemy.

THE ROAD TO RECOVERY

To overcome this pattern of pain, you and I have to lay down our carnal weapons of fear, self-defense, and hate, and pick up some righteous weapons that are effective for overcoming the lies and wounds of our true enemy. The Bible says,

> For though we live in the world, we do not wage war as the world does. The weapons we fight with

are not the weapons of the world. On the contrary, they have divine power to demolish strongholds. We demolish arguments and every pretension that sets itself up against the knowledge of God, and we take captive every thought to make it obedient to Christ.

—2 Corinthians 10:3–5, NIV

If you've been deeply hurt by another woman, you may find it difficult to imagine how you could ever move beyond the pain of your past. Maybe you don't even really want to. Maybe you have no desire for healthy female relationships. But let me encourage you to allow your pain to be a catalyst for change.

Rather than rejecting other women, why not use your righteous weapons (which have immense power) against the real enemy and watch God demolish the strongholds of your hurt?

Begin by getting involved in a local, life-giving body of believers where you can receive truth, encouragement, comfort, and safety. This is where you can begin to change your way of thinking. You will be challenged to exchange some lies for truth, to stop warring against your sisters, and to begin to redirect your strength toward the real war. Find a small group of caring girls, or even a spiritually mature woman who can walk with you.

When you can identify the propaganda, the labels, and the lies, you are ready to move forward.

If you can't find either, ask God to nurture you. Let Him mentor you. As you walk with Jesus, God can even "re-mother" you. As He heals the wounds of your past, you will begin to extend grace to others and start building a healthy attitude toward women.

With this support system in place, you can start on your road to recovery by following these steps:

Step 1: *recognize you've been fighting against your own sisters.*

Don't let your pain keep you from being honest about where you have been violated, ignored, betrayed, or wounded by women. Just because you may not want to fight doesn't mean you haven't been engaged in the war. Make a list of your offenders and pray over it. Let God show you where He wants to begin your healing.

Step 2: *identify the lies.*

Recognize the irrational or unhealthy patterns of thinking that have resulted from your painful experiences, including the lies that may have opened the door for this type of wound in the first place. When you can identify the propaganda, labels, and lies, you are ready to move forward.

Step 3: *identify the truth.*

We possess several weapons to help us in this war, but truth is one of the most important and most powerful. Plunder God's Word for His opinions, His purposes, and His promises. Surround yourself with scriptures about who you are and what God says about you. Saturate yourself in prayer, praise, and worship. Ask Him to speak the truth to you, and then listen for His answer.

Step 4: *let the truth change what you believe.*

Be patient with yourself. Truth is like a seed. You have to nurture it, take care of it, and wait for it to produce fruit. Eventually what you believe will help you form new ways of thinking, feeling, and responding. Take note of the changes you see in your heart. And don't be discouraged in your season of restoration. Soon you will see the results.

Step 5: *gather your courage and do something different.*

Break off unhealthy relationships, and begin to repair potentially positive relationships. Establish healthy boundaries that help you determine in advance what you will and won't put up with. Develop some preplanned responses to mean-spirited jabs you may receive in the future so you are prepared to be different.

. . . .

Truth is like a seed. You have to nurture it, take care of it, and wait for it to produce fruit.

. . . .

IT CAN HAPPEN TO US

Like Sarah, sometimes we think if we don't do something about our barrenness ourselves, it will never get solved. So without even asking God to direct our steps, we take charge of the situation. We implement solutions that make sense to us but wreak havoc in our homes and families. Our attempts to become fruitful only produce Ishmaels and aborted dreams. So our hearts grow disappointed. We give up hope and lose our faith. And our lives become more barren.

I do have some good news. You don't have to allow barren places to produce such despair and bitterness in you. Even out of your greatest wounds, God can cause you to be fruitful and reproduce. He can awaken your dreams, your passions, and your life-giving ability. The Lord speaks to things you thought were dead. He calls to life dreams that have been laid down, put away, or forgotten. When you choose to believe God, even in your places of barrenness, He just might birth something new through you.

• • •

QUESTIONS FOR REFLECTION

There's a lot of important work to do through the following questions. As you process, take your time. Don't get overwhelmed or discouraged. Sometimes we even have to pause and ponder some of these thoughts so we can really hear and acknowledge what God is saying. Just begin! Ask the first question, and then move forward. God is faithful and He will walk with you.

THE PATH TO HEALING

If you find yourself a "wounded warrior," there is grace and hope for you. Let's take those wounded places to God and allow Him to speak life where there has been death. Let's walk this road of recovery together and don't forget to use your journal as we move from point to point along the way.

Step 1: *recognize you've been fighting against your own sisters.*

Acknowledgement and forgiveness are powerful healers. When we acknowledge and release those who have hurt us, we not only release them, but we release ourselves from being responsible for them. When we hold on to offense and unforgiveness, we give others power over our thoughts, our feelings, and sometimes even our bodies. It's been said unforgiveness is like drinking poison and expecting the other person to die. It brings only death and destruction!

Admit you've been hurt. Ask the Lord to show you those wounded places. Make a list of the offenders. Take it to the Lord and talk with Him about how to forgive them.

Step 2: *identify the lies.*

When we are wounded, we often come to believe things about others or ourselves that aren't true—they are lies. We then live our lives as if those lies are true, shaping our behavior and coloring all of our relationships, seeing everything through the filter of those lies.

Go to the Lord in prayer and ask for His helping to see the lies for what they truly are. Use the following as a guide.

> *Father, what lies have I believed as a result of these hurts and wounds?* (Listen for His answer.) *What have I believed about other women? About me? About You?*

Step 3: *identify the truth.*

God wants to replace the lies you have believed with the truth. His truth heals the broken places in our lives, setting us free (John 8:32).

Ask Him, "God, what is the truth about [name the lie He showed you]?"

And then agree with the truth He shows you. Say the truth out loud. Write it down. Declare it!

Step 4: *let the truth change what you believe.*

Go back and review what God just said to you. Find a verse that relates and memorize it. When those painful places come up, remind yourself of the truth! The truth will set you free!

Step 5: *gather your courage and do something different.*

When we begin to understand our own wounds and that others may have them as well, we can influence our relationships for good. We can identify unhealthy relationships, repair wounded ones, and learn to set healthy boundaries.

What are some ways you can begin to do things differently with the women in your life?

List some relationships you know may need some work. How can you do things differently?

ONE FINAL THOUGHT

Barrenness is a painful condition, whether in your spiritual life or in your body. God's plan is that you would be a life-giver in all of those ways. If you've identified an area where you feel barren, let's take it to Him. Your womb—the spiritual one as well as the natural one—is designed to bring life. Use your journal and open your conversation with something like this:

> *Father, I need You. I am barren and lifeless without You. I bring You those places in me designed to produce life—and yet they haven't. I ask You to come in and touch those places. Speak life over me!*

Hearing God speak produces life. When He speaks, worlds are created and the sun gives off light (Gen. 1).

What do you hear God saying? Sometimes you need to record your impressions and thoughts. Capture what's going on inside of you and record it in your journal.

CHAPTER FOUR

A Battle Within

EXPOSING THE STRUGGLE BETWEEN FAMILY AND FRIENDS

• • •

*So I find it to be a law that when I want to do right, evil
lies close at hand. For I delight in the law of God, in my
inner being, but I see in my members another law waging
war against the law of my mind and making me captive to
the law of sin that dwells in my members. Wretched man
that I am! Who will deliver me from this body of death?*
Romans 7:21–24, ESV

It's bad enough when we are at war with a legitimate enemy
and have a righteous cause, a clear definition of victory,
and a willingness to become part of a revolution of peace.
But when the battle we wage is within our own families or
ourselves it becomes especially brutal.

We all have people in our lives who are like thorns in
our sides, continually causing us frustration. When those
"thorns" are strangers, acquaintances, or distant relatives,
we can cope with them for short periods of time. But when
the most painful people in our lives are close to us, we can't
just walk away if we don't like them or if we've been hurt by
them. Sometimes it seems as though the worst battlefields
are within our own families.

Our parents often raise us in much the same way as they were raised, never giving much thought to the significance of family behavior. Since what we grew up with is all we've ever seen or known, we tend to repeat the familiar, often passing on cycles of fear, insecurity, isolation, and comparison to our children. When these patterns of hurtful behavior combine with a cultural atmosphere that negatively portrays women and their relationships with one another, we have a "supernova" of mighty forces working against our entire gender.

> **Sometimes it seems as though the worst battlefields are within our own families.**

This passing of generational patterns isn't anything new. It has been going on as long as there have been families.

IT'S ALL IN THE FAMILY

In the Book of Genesis we read about a family filled with so much deceit and manipulation, we might be tempted to think they are different from us or even deserved the problems they had. In order to help you understand the complexity of the plot, I'm going to give you a character overview of every player in this drama. It reads like a script from a modern-day reality show.

Isaac—the father

The child of promise Sarah finally bore to Abraham in their old age grew up in a strife-filled family alongside his half-brother Ishmael and Ishmael's mom, Hagar.

When the time came for Isaac to wed, Abraham sent a servant to the land of his birth to select a bride, not wanting Isaac to marry one of the local girls. The servant did as he was instructed and found Rebekah—a stunningly beautiful virgin who exhibited a heart of service when she offered to draw water from the well for him and all his camels. The choice was confirmed when the servant learned Rebekah was related to Abraham.

When Rebekah's brother Laban saw all the jewelry and camels this servant had, he eagerly welcomed him into his home. Upon learning the purpose for his journey, Laban quickly sealed the deal, and Rebekah went with the servant to meet her groom.

Isaac and Rebekah married and, after a period of barrenness, they had two sons: Esau and Jacob. These twins were born only moments apart, and the strife between them began even before they came out of the womb.

When the boys were old enough to take wives, Isaac didn't follow his father's example and assist them in choosing women from their family line. Instead, he left this important choice to their discretion. As a result, Esau married women from the Hittite tribe, who were enemies of his ancestors. His wives treated his parents with contempt, aggression, hatred, and selfishness. "They turned out to be thorns in the sides of Isaac and Rebekah" (Gen. 26:35, THE MESSAGE).

Rebekah—the mother

When Rebekah was pregnant God told her she would have twin sons and the older one would serve his younger brother. When Esau and Jacob were grown, Rebekah took it upon herself to bring about the fulfillment of this prophecy—much like her mother-in-law, Sarah, did with Hagar. Apparently she favored Jacob; she encouraged him, the younger son, to deceive his father, Isaac, in an attempt to steal the blessing of the firstborn, which belonged to Esau.

Esau—the older brother

Esau was a rugged outdoorsman who often left camp to hunt for food for the family. He was emotionally disconnected from his mom, favored by his father, and foolishly ruled by his flesh. Upon returning from a hunting trip, particularly famished, he chose to hand over his birthright to Jacob for a bowl of soup, never pausing to consider the consequences of his actions. When he realized he had been tricked out of his inheritance, he was furious.

Jacob—the younger brother

After deceiving his father and taking advantage of his brother, Jacob fled to the land of his forefathers—in part to escape Esau, whose wrath burned against him for the treachery he and their mother had perpetuated. In his grandfather Abraham's hometown, he came to a well and saw a stunningly beautiful virgin (sound familiar?). He instantly fell in love with her. Following in the footsteps of his mother, Rebekah, Jacob watered all of Rachel's sheep. Then he told her what a miracle it was that he found her.

Rachel ran to tell her father, Laban—the same man who'd arranged for his sister Rebekah to marry Isaac. Jacob's uncle Laban warmly accepted him into his home and introduced him to his older daughter, Leah. But Jacob had eyes only for Rachel.

Upon discovering how deeply this young man loved his younger daughter, Laban struck a bargain with him. Jacob agreed to work for seven years in exchange for Rachel's hand in marriage. He was so in love with her, the years seemed like only a few days.

Laban—the father-in-law

For seven years Laban let Jacob labor in exchange for his younger daughter, knowing full well he had a responsibility to find a husband for his older daughter first. But as Jacob worked to win Rachel's hand, I imagine Laban noticed Leah falling in love with this man who did not belong to her. So Laban cooked up a plan and he enticed Leah into going along with it.

At the conclusion of Jacob's seven-year tour of duty, on the day he was to finally marry his beloved Rachel, Leah covered herself in thick veils to conceal her identity and stood before him as his bride. That night she slept with him without revealing her identity. The covenant was sealed. No annulment for Jacob.

When the deception came to light, Jacob was furious, as he had every right to be. I'd imagine Leah, after seeing the anger in her sister and in the man she hoped would desire her once he'd made love to her, was mortified and deeply shamed.

Instead of being content with the wife he'd been tricked into marrying, Jacob made a second deal with his sneaky uncle Laban. After spending the required one-week honeymoon with Leah, he immediately married Rachel too and committed to work another seven years for her.

BATTLE OF THE SISTER WIVES

At this point in the story you can feel the emotional pain and devastation of this family. The patterns of barrenness, deceit, treachery, wrath, and manipulation are nearly tangible.

The original "sister wives," Rachel and Leah spent their whole adulthood locked in a fight for the attention and affection of the same man. We don't know whether these two sisters had any serious animosity between them before Jacob came along. But you can bet they exchanged a whole lot of hurtful barbs from that point on.

"I had him before you did."

"Only because you and Father tricked him."

"I'm his first wife."

"Yeah, well, I'm the one he really loves."

And Jacob, who'd deceived both his father and his brother, was now the victim of deceit himself.

Leah—the first wife

Leah desperately hoped Jacob would come to love her, even though she knew his affections were for her sister and despite the fact she'd chosen to cooperate with Laban in tricking him into this union. Instead Jacob emotionally disconnected himself from her. The combination of guilt, disappointment, and rejection was painful. Yet God saw Leah in the midst of this mess and had compassion on her.

> When God realized that Leah was unloved, he opened her womb.
> —Genesis 29:31, THE MESSAGE

Leah gave birth to four sons in quick succession. We can tell by the names she gave them Leah loved Jacob desperately and longed for his approval, attention, and affection. She hoped Jacob would love her because of these boys (Gen. 29:33–35).

The first son was named Reuben, which means, "It's a boy." After his birth, Leah said, "Now my husband will love me."

The second son was Simon, which means "God heard."

Levi means "Connect." Following his birth, Leah said, "Now my husband will connect with me."

It wasn't until the birth of her fourth child that Leah shifted from a desire for Jacob to a desire for God. His name was Judah, which means "Praise God." After that she stopped having children for a long season. Why? Apparently Jacob stopped sleeping with her.

Rachel—the second wife

While her sister had baby after baby, Rachel remained barren. This painful inability to produce offspring of her own further enhanced the brutality of the competition between the sisters. Rachel allowed her jealousy to take the form of bitterness. Finally she told Jacob, "Give me children, or I will die" (Gen. 30:1, MEV), as if he had the power to open her womb.

Rachel was so distraught over her barrenness, she offered her maid, Bilhah, to serve as a surrogate mother (just as Abraham's wife, Sarah, did with her maid, Hagar). Bilhah gave birth to children on Rachel's behalf, and their names reflect the depth of Rachel's bitterness, aimed squarely at her sister (Gen. 30:6–8).

Dan means "vindication."

Naphtali means "fight." Following his birth, Rachel said, "I've been in an all-out fight with my sister—and I've won."

Since Leah couldn't seem to win Jacob's affection, she responded to Rachel's hateful barbs by offering her maid, Zilpah, as a surrogate mother. Zilpah had two boys: Gad, which means "lucky," and Asher, meaning "happy."

For a while, no one in Jacob's family had any children.

So Rachel struck a bargain with Leah. In exchange for some mandrakes, which were thought to aid in conception, Rachel offered a night of intimacy with their husband.

I wonder how Jacob felt about this exchange. Apparently he chose to enter into the agreement, because Leah conceived again—twice. She gave Jacob two more boys: Issachar, meaning, "bartered," and Zebulon, meaning, "honor."

Even after giving her husband six sons, Leah still longed for Jacob's approval and love. And even with her husband's preferential love, Rachel still ached to bear a child.

"Then God remembered Rachel. God listened to her and opened her womb" (Gen. 30:22, THE MESSAGE). Finally, after years of barrenness and bitterness, Rachel became pregnant and had a son. She named him Joseph, saying, "God has taken away my humiliation." Rachel felt vindicated by Joseph's birth, but she was not satisfied. She prayed for one more son, and God answered her request. This last child, Benjamin (meaning "son of hope"), entered the world at the cost of her life.

CYCLES AND PATTERNS

If we're not careful we'll unconsciously fall into the same traps Sarah, Jacob, Rachel, Leah, and Esau did. We'll handle disagreements with treachery, use manipulation to get our way, even long for love that is not meant for us. We'll try to force others into fulfilling our dreams. If we don't wake up to these generational patterns, we'll unknowingly continue the cycles of abuse and pain.

While I was growing up, my dad often worked two jobs to provide me with cheerleading uniforms, dance lessons, and special gifts. In many ways he was my hero, a gentle man who left me with a strong work ethic and many happy memories. Yet he so despised conflict he would avoid it at almost any cost. In my teen years some type of falling-out happened between him and his mom and seemingly overnight there was a cutting off of the relationship. My father passed away in 2001 without seeing a restoration with his mother. His method of dealing with difficult relationships had a strong impact on me. I often found myself tempted to resolve conflict by withdrawing from the fight and rejecting other people.

If we don't wake up to these generational patterns, we'll unknowingly continue the cycles of abuse and pain.

My mom's side of the family had what I call "love-hate" relationships. They would be so excited to get together, but then it seemed they couldn't wait to get apart! The atmosphere with my mom's family was always loud and often tense. Everyone had high expectations about how they should act; as a result, they had lots of practice disappointing one another, especially the women. It's not that they didn't love each other. They just loved harshly and in some ways dangerously. We weren't violent, but rather emotionally vulnerable and prone to wounding. As a young woman I often chose to ignore the painful parts of our family life rather than work on overcoming them. I learned early how to avoid conflict, run from a tense conversation, and behave in ways that were classic "people pleasing." In the early years of my marriage I often isolated myself from my family, especially my parents, dealing them some painful daughter wounds. Many years went by before I was mature enough to recognize my own sinful ways or brave enough to both seek and receive forgiveness.

A few years ago I was asked to write an article for the women's magazine at Gateway Church, *Studio G*. I wrote about my vision and hope for healthy female relationships. To illustrate my points, I included a little bit of detail about my personal history, including my perceptions of the love-hate relationships between the women in my family as I was growing up.

When my mom read the article, it hurt her feelings. Discovering how I remembered some of my childhood, and how I related certain aspects of our family, opened up a vulnerable place in my mom's heart and in her own memories. After all, it's one thing to talk privately about your family dynamics. It's another to write about them for all to see.

When my mom told me how the article made her feel, I was grieved to learn my comments had hurt her. My insensitivity was a reflection of the very patterns of behavior I was trying to expose. Thankfully it gave me an opportunity to apologize and us a chance to honestly acknowledge some things we'd never discussed.

Over the next few months we started to talk about some of the painful patterns in our family, including the way the women spoke to and related with one another. Then one day, like a fog suddenly lifting, we recognized we had a bent toward harshness in our family, especially in our female relationships. We tended to be hard on one another, quick to judge, and slow to forgive. Over the years, both my mother and I had responded to our painful experiences in inappropriate ways.

Once we recognized these patterns in our family, we realized we could change them. So can you. We have the power within ourselves to alter the course of our future.

The memories you have of how your family relates and the patterns of how they interact with one another is like a massive, deep river. Your history can be a current of blessings or of curses. Either way, it has tremendous momentum.

Once we recognized these patterns in our family line, we realized we could change them. We had the power within ourselves to alter the course of our future.

The only way to change the flow from curse to blessing is to build a dam, which intersects the momentum and redirects its course. The first person in a family line to do so will experience a tremendous amount of pressure. The tide of our patterns tends to lead us toward a particular destination, like the force of a river current. However, we can create a way for the release of a different legacy and the formation of a new pattern.

The day my mom and I took a stand, we began to establish a new direction for the future of our family. She became a first-generation dam builder and, as I stood with her in prayer, I became the second generation. Together we are forging a way for my children to be third-generation builders of peace and love. We can't do all the work for them, but they now have a different leaning—one that can release the blessings God has in store for them and for their children.

My mom exercised great courage that day. She could have denied my memories were true, or tried to diminish the importance of what I saw in our family heritage. Instead she did the work necessary to turn a curse into a blessing. I consider myself greatly blessed to be so loved and to have witnessed the change in direction for the future of our family.

You can be the first person to change the tide of war within your own family. Step into the river. Stand in the gap. Yield to forgiveness. Fight for the truth. Then your children, and your children's children, will be at peace.

• • •

QUESTIONS FOR REFLECTION

What about your family? Do you sense a current you'd like to embrace or one you'd like to change? Maybe you are like me, seeing patterns you don't like and finding you express yourself in a way that harms others. I think I was a little like a bull in a china closet. I just wanted it to be different so badly. You can learn from my mistakes. Let's walk through the following questions together, giving thoughtful consideration to our family history. I believe God will help you to navigate the fast-flowing water in a way that will allow you to embrace the good and redirect the negative without harming others. Grab your journal and let's get started.

Sarah, Rebekah, and Rachel all had promises from the Lord regarding their families. Yet all three of them took matters into their own hands, and resorted to deception and manipulation to achieve what they wanted. How did this affect future generations of their families?

How did God deal with these women, despite their faults? What principles can you draw upon, as you desire to become more life-giving in your own female relationships?

"Once we recognized these patterns in our family, we realized we could change them."

What patterns (negative or positive) have you observed in your own family? Are there any patterns you'd like to change? Record those in your journal.

Ask God to help you identify some relationships in your family that might need some healing. Are there some ways you might be able to begin to turn the tide in your own family?

Have you had any opportunities to have a discussion similar to the one my mom and I had? What about with a friend or coworker? Describe those conversations.

You can be the first person to change the tide of war in your family and leave your children a legacy of peace. Will you decide today to be that person in your family? What relationships can you take steps to repair that could have a long-term and multi-generational impact?

CHAPTER FIVE

Missing in Action

WOUNDS THAT MAKE US PRISONERS OF WAR

• • •

*Though an army should encamp against me, my
heart will not fear; though war should rise
against me, in this will I be confident.*
Psalm 27:3, MEV

One of the most dreadful experiences a soldier can experience is becoming a prisoner of war. When enemy forces capture a soldier he is deprived of his liberty. Although international laws exist to prevent abuse of prisoners of war, they are often isolated, tortured, starved, or mentally abused. They can lose their sense of identity and even become confused about who is their enemy.

When I look into the face of a woman who has been trapped by lies and patterns of abuse, it often seems she has been taken hostage. Even if she tries hard, she doesn't really feel good about herself. She often yearns for love, but finds it's never enough. No matter how many sexual relationships she engages in, she can't seem to stop the general sense of unwellness and disconnection. She longs for comfort but can't receive it. She doesn't relate to others with confidence. She knows something's wrong, but she can't identify the problem. She is captured like a prisoner of war. She is missing in action. And she may not even know who is her enemy.

Many factors may affect such a woman, including painful past experiences and family issues. But her real enemy is Satan. He has the audacity to try to capture her heart and mind. He turns woman against woman, mother against her children. Many of our sisters are snared in his traps.

CIRCLE OF LIFE

When my kids were young, the movie *The Lion King* was a huge hit. It became one of the most successful Broadway musicals, was produced in high school drama departments around the nation, and has recently been rereleased in 3-D. I love this story and its music, especially the song "Circle of Life."

This song plays as the background to a very important scene where the Lion King's infant son, Simba, is presented to the nation. Animals of every kind come to show their respect and to honor the youngest member of the royal family. A special blessing is publicly declared, an acknowledgement of the cub's royal destiny. All of this happens to a backdrop of inspiring music and a crescendo of emotion.

When I look into the face of a woman who has been trapped by lies, generational curses, and patterns of abuse, it often seems she has been taken hostage.

I wish this were how we welcomed all of our offspring. Few of us are presented to the world with this kind of fanfare. How many people actually have a whole tribe show up soon after they are born to declare their purpose and potential? Was the day of your birth marked with such acceptance and hope? Or did you get off to more of a bumpy start?

BELOVED DAUGHTER

In God's divine plan there is a "circle of life." You and I are supposed to be daughters first. We are to be protected, valued, encouraged, and cherished. We are a gift and a reward: the apple of our fathers' eyes, and the pride and joy of our mothers. From this place of love and acceptance, we can go on to be sisters, then wives, then mothers and grandmothers, cheerfully and gratefully passing on our heritage to the next generation, perpetuating our own unique circle of life.

But what happens when the first role of your life is negatively affected? Satan wants to subvert our lives at an early age and convince us we are unloved so he can get us off track from the very beginning. This is why he doesn't wait until we're grown to try to destroy our destiny. He strikes his most intentional and often effective blows at our very first female relationship, the relationship with our mother.

The mother-daughter bond is the first woman-to-woman relationship in a girl's life, and it's critical to the shaping and development of her character and self-image. From our moms we learn to trust, to love, and to be loved. We develop patterns of intimacy, learn how to relate to others, and even discover how to properly separate from our mothers—all components of emotional maturity.

Moms who are physically or emotionally sick or absent do tremendous damage to their children, leaving them with a sense of abandonment and a lack of safety. Many of us grew up in an environment that lacked the most basic human needs: love and peace. As a result, our souls can become pockmarked with tender sores and open wounds.

I am so sad when I learn of a woman who has grown up under the influence of a mom who was deeply wounded herself. You may have been unwanted or even abandoned. You might have lost your mother to sickness or death. Or perhaps you were simply overlooked or left out. You may have had to grow up too fast and assume responsibilities far beyond your ability or maturity. Maybe you were physically abused or verbally assaulted. These wounds are formed from human sin, weakness, and the wounds the abuser herself may be carrying.

From our moms we learn to trust, to love, and to be loved.

But not all wounds are forged from neglect, selfishness, sickness, or evil. Even good moms and healthy families who do their best can wound us unintentionally and leave some marks on the development of a child's heart.

Author Gary Chapman, in his series of books about the five "love languages," explains how every person has a primary way of showing and receiving love.[1] Let's say your mom's primary love language is "acts of service." Because she loves you, she spends her entire life serving you. She prepares healthy meals, welcomes your friends into the home, signs you up for extracurricular activities, chauffeurs you everywhere, does your laundry, helps you with homework, etc.

But let's say your love language is "words of affirmation." As an adult, you find yourself saying, "I can't remember my mother ever telling me, 'I love you.'" Your mom might have bent over backward to show her love for you, but because she didn't do it in the way that meant the most to you, you feel unloved.

The lack of a positive mom relationship can leave you with a sense of perpetual loss, emptiness, and emotional disconnect. We try to soothe our souls with anything that will relieve the pain. This makes us susceptible to a number of coping mechanisms, including addictions, manipulation, apathy, overachieving, isolation, and abandonment.

Negative mothering can establish a pattern of mistrust for the rest of our lives. We learn to hide our needs, or try to meet them on our own or through inappropriate measures. We become vulnerable. We don't feel safe or accepted. This creates a breeding ground for insecurity and fear, and sometimes the fruit of this upbringing is negativity and aggressiveness.

If your first female relationship is lacking in nurture, it will produce a wound in your spirit that will critically shape your development, your character, and how you feel about yourself and other women.

CHERISHED SISTER

The second most significant woman-to-woman relationship most of us experience is with our sisters and the girls we grow up with. They can be our biological sisters, a close relative like an aunt or cousin, or even a dear friend. A sister could be defined as any woman who walks closely with you. That's where we get the saying, "She's like a sister to me."

Our siblings, whether biological or not, give us our first taste of community. We have a sense that we belong in this "family," where there are others like us. We learn we are different but still somehow the same. Ideally we grow old together and find a lifelong friend and advocate within our homes.

But it's not always like that.

Far too often we engage in "sister wars." A younger sibling resents growing up in her older sister's shadow, always feeling one-upped or a step behind. A firstborn child may feel jealousy over all the attention given to the baby of the family or be irritated about always having to take care of her younger brothers and sisters. If a parent shows favoritism toward one child, seeming to prefer one to the other, it will create an even greater division.

Maybe you and your sister were friends as children, but something seemingly unforgiveable came between you. Maybe she told lies about you or stole your boyfriend, and the two of you ended up in a bitter, never-ending feud. Now there is no pulling together for a greater good, no one to pick you up when you fall. And no one to rejoice with you when you're happy or weep with you when you're sad.

In addition, you can easily develop an attitude of competition. Sisters are constantly tempted to compare themselves. Each one strives to get her own needs met, even at the cost of the other. This builds a sense of isolation and loneliness. Competition and rejection create a cycle of emotional trauma that shapes our viewpoint and expectations for years.

The lack of a positive mom relationship can leave you with a sense of perpetual loss, emptiness, and emotional disconnect.

Because sisters (or childhood best friends) grow up side by side, they are capable of making wounds that are especially deep and painful. A mean-spirited sibling is dangerous because you don't naturally shield your heart from someone who should be safe. She knows your strengths and your weaknesses, so even a casual remark or oversight can become a barb that comes swiftly and penetrates deeply. This only needs to happen a few times before you protect yourself, developing a defensive attitude and a quick trigger of rejection.

As adults we come to realize this is unhealthy, but we don't know how to change. We may want to just walk away from a sister. But our family ties keep us coming back to the same patterns of pain year after year. We face the choice of repeating those patterns or simply turning our backs on the relationships. Many families have been irrevocably broken because sisters did not know how to forge a new relationship with each other and begin again.

TREASURED FRIEND

We all share a basic human need to be accepted and loved by people. Friends are people we choose to allow into our lives. We form bonds with them, creating relationships characterized (I hope) by vulnerability and trust. Close friendship is more than comfortable companionship. It helps us with our blind spots, reveals our weaknesses, and supports us as we overcome our failings. We are accepted. We are loved. We are valuable. A real friend can tell us the truth because we've given her permission to do so. This combination of attachment and truth, if developed in love, allows us to see ourselves as we really are, grow in our emotional health, and learn we matter. When others receive us just as we are, we are better equipped to cope with the ups and downs of life.

Many families have been irrevocably broken because sisters did not know how to forge a new relationship with each other and begin again.

Most of us enter our school-age years with a sense of trepidation. We're not sure how the others will respond to us. We don't know if we will be accepted. We strive to fit in by finding our "tribe," and we long to be recognized by them. If our first friendships are marked with mistrust or failure, we grow insecure and wary. If we have experiences, both in the home and in our extended relationships, that are wounding, we grow up believing something is wrong with us.

As we enter adolescence, we want to differentiate ourselves from the crowd. Girls start competing with one another for the attention of boys. We compare ourselves, one to another, in areas such as physical appearance or popularity with peers. This creates an environment of striving and backbiting, sometimes leading to tearing others down to build up our own self-esteem. Our own insecurity makes us easily susceptible to failed friendships.

We soon learn there is power in our femininity. People respond differently to us based on how we present ourselves. If we are desperate to get attention or to be loved, we may use our sex appeal for attention and influence. We might even reject other women in order to exalt ourselves. In our attempt to protect our own hearts, we do and say horrible things to one another.

As a young wife my friend Beth realized all of her female friends had known one another since childhood. These women enjoyed all-girl getaway weekends and monthly girls' nights out. When Beth was invited to join them, she went. But the events always left her feeling insecure and jealous—and realizing how much she missed out on by not having developed childhood friendships.

My friend Kelly often joked that when she was growing up, her family moved every time the rent was due. She has at least two report cards from different schools for every grade throughout elementary school to prove it. As soon as she became friends with someone, it was time to move again.

Her family finally settled in one place when Kelly was eleven years old. Although she welcomed the stability, by this time a hard shell had formed over her heart and she continued exercising her coping mechanisms. Her defenses were locked and loaded, and her walls remained high and thick.

When we cannot find answers for our pain, we reproduce the cycle of abuse. Those who have been wounded become wounders themselves.

During another friend's teenage years, many of her friendships were laced with mistrust, ulterior motives, and manipulation. So her guard went up. She wanted to have—and to be—a loyal friend. But she always kept herself at a safe distance. Even now as an adult, she has trouble finding and trusting friends.

DIVORCE

Some of us never get over this awkward season. We enter the greater world of grown-ups with a general lack of safety, unsure how other women are going to respond to us. As our painful experiences and broken relationships accumulate, we respond with what seems like a rational solution: to build walls around our hearts. When we cannot find answers for our pain, we reproduce the cycle of abuse. Those who have been wounded become wounders themselves. As we injure the people around us, they respond by withdrawing from us.

We learn to make snap decisions about people. We pass them through the screen of our judgment, evaluate their threat level, and make assumptions about their motives. Essentially, we put on other women what is really in us: fear and mistrust. The judgments and generalizations we make hinder our ability to connect, thereby perpetuating a circle of emotional death.

If you're healthy and someone hurts you, you can go to her and say, "Hey, that hurt." If the other person is also healthy, she'll probably say something like, "I'm sorry. I didn't mean to hurt you." There can be speedy exposure of the pain, quick forgiveness, and full and immediate restoration of the friendship.

But if you're unhealthy and wounded, when you hit a bump in a relationship, it will seem like a mountain. Instead of attempting to work through it, you turn away and try to ignore it. Offenses stack up, and pretty soon you get sick of the whole thing. You no longer want to continue the relationship. So you break up. It's almost like you get a divorce.

Divorce is a total separation, the breaking of a union. We usually think of it in terms of marriage, but there are all kinds of relationships that can be broken.

You can "divorce" your girlfriends or your mother or a sister. I know parents who haven't seen their children in years. Even church congregations can split.

AN ORPHAN SPIRIT

If the lies surrounding your wounds have convinced you that you are unloved and unwanted, you have effectively become an orphan, feeling utterly abandoned and alone. Those who suffer with an orphan spirit don't feel they can depend on others. They believe they are totally alone and no one really knows or loves them. They have to fight for everything they get because there isn't enough to go around. They are plagued by thoughts like, "Nobody loves me. I don't really matter. I have to take care of myself because no one else will."

The enemy wants you to believe the lie you are orphaned and alone, a prisoner of war, beyond the reach of loved ones.

Orphans are often invisible in the midst of a crowd. They look, sound, and act normal, fitting in often because they have developed strong coping patterns.

One way of dealing with an orphan spirit is to become a people pleaser. Those who use this survival mechanism strive for early success and approval, sometimes even becoming successful leaders. They morph their personalities to fit the expectations of others, often being taken advantage of. As a result, they don't set proper boundaries, lose touch with their own desires, and aren't really sure what they want. They don't know who they are or why what they have to offer never seems to be enough.

Others try to cope with their sense of abandonment

by self-medicating with drugs, alcohol, work, or sex. This is how addictions are formed. These people try to alleviate anxiety and stress through temporary management of their emotions or by hyperfocus of their energy. They build a thick wall around their hearts, and they effectively suppress all painful emotions. As a result they become lethargic, apathetic, exhausted, and emotionally disconnected.

The enemy wants you to believe the lie that you are orphaned and alone, a prisoner of war, beyond the reach of loved ones. He wants to convince you that even your heavenly Father couldn't possibly love someone like you.

Nothing could be further from the truth. Psalm 139:13–18 (NIV) illustrates how deeply God has always cared for you, even before you were born.

> You created my inmost being; you knit me together in my mother's womb. I praise you because I am fearfully and wonderfully made; your works are wonderful, I know that full well. My frame was not hidden from you when I was made in the secret place. When I was woven together in the depths of the earth, your eyes saw my unformed body. All the days ordained for me were written in your book before one of them came to be. How precious to me are your thoughts, O God! How vast is the sum of them! Were I to count them, they would outnumber the grains of sand—when I awake, I am still with you.

Everything about you is wonderfully fashioned with care and purpose by God. From the moment of your conception, you have been known and loved by your heavenly Father. You have not been abandoned or forsaken. Neither the circumstances of your birth nor the dysfunction of your relationships can separate you from His all-encompassing love. Everything that you see as broken or rejected, He sees as redeemed.

> **Everything that you see as broken or rejected, He sees as redeemed.**

Just when you fear you have reached the end of yourself or your circumstances, you will find God faithful. You are not alone. You are not orphaned. You have not been left on the battlefield or abandoned as a prisoner of war. You have the perfect parent, the perfect sibling, and the perfect friend in our Savior, Jesus Christ. You are destined to be rescued and to become a daughter of God.

• • •

QUESTIONS FOR REFLECTION

Take a deep breath with me. In this chapter, we've explored some of our most intimate and vulnerable relationships. You may have stumbled upon some places of deep wounding. I want to encourage you to once again take the time to process what you are learning with God. Use your journal to document your memories, experiences, and feelings. It's OK if you need to seek some help with these revelations. Reach out to a friend or even a Christian counselor.

Don't isolate yourself or become fearful. God will help you move forward through this process and receive healing. Let's work together.

I described a woman who is a prisoner of war this way:

> Even if she tries hard, she doesn't really feel good about herself. She often yearns for love, but finds it's never enough. No matter how many sexual relationships she engages in, she can't seem to stop the general sense of unwellness and disconnection. She longs for comfort but can't receive it. She doesn't relate to others with confidence. She knows something's wrong, but she can't identify the problem. She is captured like a prisoner of war. She is missing in action. And she may not even know who is her enemy.

Do you see yourself in any part of this description? If so, explain.

Can you identify other women who also demonstrate some of these characteristics? What could you do to reach out to them? Is there anything you would change about your own response to them, if you understood this pattern more clearly? Please explain.

Perhaps from your very birth, the enemy has come against your identity as cherished daughter, cherished sister, and treasured friend. He has sought to fracture those female relationships and leave you orphaned. But God has a bigger plan. Let's ask Him.

God, what relationships have been broken in my life? [Write down what He shows you.] *Father, because of this brokenness, I feel _____. When _____ happened, it made me feel _____.*

Be open. Wait. Listen. Write down anyone who comes to mind. Then remember our work on forgiveness from the previous chapters and respond:

Lord, today I choose to forgive _____. I release them, and I give them to You. I choose to let go of the pain they have caused me. I invite You to heal my broken heart and to teach me about being Your daughter. Restore to me a circle of life.

Can you identify with feeling like an orphan? Write down the situations or memories that make you feel abandoned or alone.

"You are not alone. You are not orphaned. You have not been left alone on the battlefield or abandoned as a prisoner of war."

Read Psalm 139:13–16 out loud. Allow the Lord to heal those wounded places and speak to you. Journal your thoughts and feelings.

CHAPTER SIX

A Broken Branch

MOTHERS RESTORE LIFE AND BRING PEACE

• • •

I am the vine, you are the branches. He who remains in Me, and I in him, bears much fruit. For without Me you can do nothing.
John 15:5, MEV

There are five active-duty branches of the United States armed services: Marine Corps, Navy, Army, Air Force, and Coast Guard. Each branch is an equal part of the US military, all headed by the president as commander-in-chief. They all have specific assignments in relationship to the protection and care of our nation, its people, and the world. Their first responsibility is to serve as peacekeeping forces.

The Marines are known for their bravery and brotherhood, often being the first on the ground in combat situations. The Navy defends our rights to travel and trade freely on the world's oceans. The Army is the oldest branch and serves to protect the security of the United States and its resources. The Air Force focuses on guarding American interests through strategic placement and deployment of air power. The Coast Guard secures the American waterways, and during wartime it deploys in partnership with the Navy.

Can you imagine the threat to our national security if even one of these branches were incapacitated? We'd be wide open to the threat of our enemies. No measure of homeland security or scrambling of the other branches could sufficiently ensure our safety.

You could say the same of our family trees. They contain a group of major branches, with numerous offshoots. Each child represents a new branch that grows wide and strong as that child marries and has children of his or her own. Each division of the tree has special assignments and focused responsibilities. When all the branches are full and functioning, we experience peace. If one of those branches is devastated, we suffer tremendous loss.

YOUR TREE

Have you ever tried to trace your family tree? People who love genealogies spend many enjoyable hours poring over historical records in order to chart the various lines of their ancestry, whether biological or by marriage or adoption. It can be interesting to discover what famous people might be in your lineage. And often the most fascinating aspect of this hobby is coming across stories written by distant relatives describing what their lives were like.

Most family trees have a few branches here and there that suddenly stop. A line of descendants culminates in a child who had no offspring, perhaps never married, and maybe even died before reaching an age where he or she could reproduce. These "stumps" in the family tree bring a touch of sadness to our hearts as we wonder what might have been. We imagine how much fuller our tree—and our lives—could have been if our line had continued instead of being stunted.

I often imagine that in the very deepest part of myself, the place where the Holy Spirit resides, there is a beautiful tree of life. It was a seed at the moment of my salvation, and as my life is touched, healed, and transformed by my love affair with Him, the seed becomes a beautiful oak. My tree is supposed to grow strong and provide shade, protection, food, and even fresh seed for those near to me.

If you have a significant woman wound, it is as if one huge branch of your tree was broken off and didn't grow. There is a stump in the place where there is meant to be comfort, shade, and beauty for others to enjoy. Your tree is still supported by its root system and may be fruitful in other areas, but this branch remains damaged. It's like part of your family tree where a generational line of your ancestry suddenly ends, leaving a broken spot on your graph. You're left wondering what blessings might have come from this part of your life if only this wound hadn't killed this portion of your tree.

If you have a significant woman wound, it is as if one huge branch of your tree was broken off and didn't grow.

You aren't the only one. All of us were born like Eve, sharing in the sin and consequences of the war we wage with our enemy. Every woman's internal tree has suffered damage and been marred by the consequences of this battle.

But this is not the end of the story. There is another woman—another mother—for us to consider. Her name was Mary.

THE BIRTH OF LOVE

Have you ever wondered why God chose Mary to be the mother of Jesus? What made her so special? What were her qualifications for this lofty position? Since she was just a teen at the time, she hadn't had many opportunities to do great things for God or to demonstrate mountain-moving faith.

Yet God entrusted His entire plan of salvation to her. God didn't just send Jesus to us—He placed the Savior of the world in the womb of an unwed teenage girl. As a result Mary had an opportunity to do what Eve was unable to do. Instead of birthing hate, she birthed love.

As the story unfolds in Luke 1, we find God sent an angel, Gabriel, to deliver a message to Mary. He found her in her hometown of Nazareth, where she was engaged to be married to Joseph.

Gabriel opened the conversation by calling Mary "highly favored" and noting the Lord was with her. Mary was immediately troubled, so much so that Gabriel encouraged her not to be afraid. Then he revealed the real purpose of his visit:

> You will conceive and give birth to a son, and you will name him Jesus. He will be very great and will be called the Son of the Most High. The Lord

God will give him the throne of his ancestor David.
And he will reign over Israel forever; his Kingdom
will never end!
—Luke 1:31–33

This message was enough information for Mary to
understand two things: 1) the angel was talking about her
carrying a natural baby, and 2) the baby would be the long-
awaited Messiah.

**All of us were born like Eve, sharing in the sin and
consequences of the war we wage with our enemy.**

Mary didn't argue about whether she was favored or
wonder if she might be hallucinating. She didn't even point
out the obvious reasons she was probably not the right
choice for this assignment. She simply asked, "How will
this be...since I am a virgin?" (Luke 1:34, NIV).

The angel replied, "The Holy Spirit will come upon you,
and the power of the Most High will overshadow you. So
the baby to be born will be holy, and he will be called the
Son of God" (Luke 1:35).

This answer must have blown her mind. It blows mine!

Mary could have said no. Everything in the natural
would have urged her to decline this assignment. She
wasn't married. She was too young. She'd never been with
a man. This would have been totally contrary to the plans
she had for her life. And I'm certain she did not consider
herself qualified to be the mother of the Messiah.

Yet Mary said yes.

As a matter of fact, she said yes multiple times and in the most beautiful of ways.

AGREE

Mary was very young, at the beginning of her childbearing years. Being engaged, she was no doubt looking forward to becoming a wife and a mother. But when the angel visited her, her plans turned to dust. God had a different plan. And when Mary first heard it, she could have been filled with fear for her future.

Instead she responded, "I am the Lord's servant. May everything you have said about me come true" (Luke 1:38).

Mary could have aborted God's plan by declining to partner in His purposes. But her heart said yes. I believe this is why God chose her.

Mary evaluated the magnitude, the unlikeliness, and the personal cost of the angel's message and made a decision to receive this assignment. Her willing response became the seedbed of life for generations to come.

When Elizabeth and Mary conceived, they received not only a deposit of life, but also a gift of faith.

God values our ability to give life so much that He laid aside all of His deity and became an infant, completely vulnerable to the care of a teenage girl. He entrusted Himself to a fully human mother.

You too can carry a prophetic promise. The fulfillment of God's plans for you and your family tree begins with your willingness. Whatever He is asking you to do; it is your "yes" that allows Him to deposit something divine and powerful within you. Saying yes may cost you something. It may cost everything you hold dear. But the blessings He has in store for you will far outweigh anything you might give up.

What dreams are you carrying in the womb of your spirit? What does God desire to accomplish through you? How many goals have you aborted because you came up with a list of reasons and excuses instead of simply saying yes to Him? God has good plans for you, a hope and future (Jer. 29:11). Will you choose to receive them?

BELIEVE

With the angel's words still ringing in her ears and pounding in her heart, Mary rushed to see her cousin Elizabeth.

Throughout her prime childbearing years, Elizabeth was barren. But when Gabriel visited Mary, he informed her Elizabeth had become pregnant in her old age and was already in her sixth month. Through a supernatural act, she too was carrying a child of promise. Who better to understand Mary's predicament?

The moment Mary arrived at her cousin's home, the baby in Elizabeth's womb leapt. Elizabeth immediately saw the call and destiny on Mary's life and rejoiced with her. There was no e-mail, text, or Facebook message that let Elizabeth in on this little secret. By the Holy Spirit she recognized the blessing on Mary's life and she knew Mary had been chosen as the mother of the Messiah. Seeing Mary's faith, she said, "Blessed is she who believed" (Luke 1:45, MEV).

Whatever He is asking you to do; it is your "yes" that allows Him to deposit something divine and powerful within you.

Elizabeth and Mary both carried children of destiny. Each woman had a divine conception and a controversial pregnancy. And they both paid a high price for the privilege of carrying these children. These women faced an immediate social consequence, but ultimately each of them had to give her child fully to his destiny. John the Baptist and Jesus were both killed for their faith. Yet their deaths were the seedbed of eternal life for you and me. Everything stolen in the garden was restored to us through the death and resurrection of Jesus.

When Elizabeth and Mary conceived, they received not only a deposit of life, but also a gift of faith. This faith gave them the grace to accomplish what God was asking them to do. Supernatural intimacy sparked supernatural faith, which gave them the capacity to receive life and carry it to fruition.

For three months Elizabeth mentored Mary. Mary found in her an older woman she could receive encouragement from, even someone she could celebrate with.

Do you need an Elizabeth in your life? Don't wait for one to come to you. Mary didn't sit at home pining for someone who could relate to her. She went to her cousin, even though the journey took a few days.

Do you know someone who could use an Elizabeth? Don't turn her away. Welcome her into your life with open arms and speak words of encouragement to her heart.

PRAISE

Having trekked across the mountains to get to her cousin's house, Mary had some time to think about the consequences of her encounter with the angel. She could easily have given in to fear at this point. Yet instead she chose to praise the Lord, exalt His virtues, and esteem His purpose and plan:

> My soul glorifies the Lord and my spirit rejoices in God my Savior, for he has been mindful of the humble state of his servant. From now on all generations will call me blessed, for the Mighty One has done great things for me—holy is his name. His mercy extends to those who fear him, from generation to generation. He has performed mighty deeds with his arm; he has scattered those who are proud in their inmost thoughts.
>
> He has brought down rulers from their thrones but has lifted up the humble. He has filled the hungry with good things, but has sent the rich away empty. He has helped his servant Israel, remembering to be merciful to Abraham and his descendants forever, just as he promised our ancestors.
>
> —Luke 1:46–55, NIV

Mary's praise sustained her in the days ahead. This declaration, made before she knew the full measure of the consequences of her cooperation, became her life story. It spoke acceptance to the baby in her womb, positioning her to carry life within her young body. As a result, you and I are among the generations who call her "blessed."

The difference between them is not in their capacity. The difference lies in whom they listened to.

LISTEN

Eve and Mary were both destined to become life-givers. Each was handpicked by God to be the mother of all living. The difference between them is not in their capacity. The difference lies in whom they listened to.

Eve could have spoken to God about her concerns, or even to Adam. Instead she talked with a cunning serpent and reasoned herself into disobedience.

Mary had questions, just like Eve. She was trying to reason in her mind how this could be. But she chose to discuss what God said to her with Gabriel and Elizabeth. The angel responded to her concerns based on the prophetic promise over her life. She took counsel from an angel of the Lord. Then she ran to another mother—a relative and friend. And there she found comfort, hope, and celebration.

Who are you listening to? Are you communing with an angelic messenger or entertaining the thoughts and reasoning of the enemy? Are you willing to seek the encouragement and support of another woman so she can breathe life into you and your dreams?

HOW'S YOUR BRANCH?

Eve and Mary both had the seeds for a tree of life. Yet one birthed hate and the other birthed love.

Remember the tree-of-life illustration I shared earlier in this chapter? What does your tree look like? Is it a big, beautiful oak of righteousness that ministers to a lot of people? Or does your tree have some blighted branches that need the redemption that comes through Christ?

Do not be discouraged because of your wounds. Lean toward the Lord in your need and He will comfort you. He will speak to you, and He will reveal Himself to you. Overcome your pain by offering a huge measure of thankfulness that will sustain you like a life raft. An appreciative heart is developed through a disciplined, purposeful decision of your will to give thanks regardless of the circumstances.

Can a broken branch be repaired? Our Father is the master at pruning what has become barren. He will take what we think is just an ugly stump and use it to produce abundant fruit. The place in you that has been dormant can live again. The moment you choose to listen to the truth and run toward a woman who will celebrate your unique destiny, call out your faith, and challenge you to praise God, your tree will grow again.

• • •

QUESTIONS FOR REFLECTION

I am grateful God didn't leave us in our fallen state. Rather, He had a plan all along to redeem us and to restore us to our original design. Mary did us all a big favor by going first. Now you and I have a responsibility—an opportunity— to say yes to the invitation of God to partner with Him to bring life and healing to others. As we begin to dig into the solutions and the good news of God's strategy, take time to praise Him for what He's already done on your behalf. Then pull up to my kitchen table, grab your journal and a cup of coffee, and let's talk.

Have you ever looked up your family tree? What interesting people or stories did you find?

What does your "tree of life" look like? Are there full, rich, shady parts? Stumps? If you have some broken places in your heart that feel like stumps, you may need to grieve what could have been. Take time to journal about those places. Express your loss and ask the Holy Spirit to comfort you. Don't rush by the pain but rather submit it to God. Use your journal as a tool to help you process.

Like Mary, there can be a prophetic promise in you. It will begin to blossom and grow as you are able to say yes to God's purpose. Take a minute and consider the prophetic promise God wants to deposit in you.

Is there something you are passionate about? Is there someone you long to serve or reach? Is there a sense of destiny upon your life? Ask God about His plans for you and journal what you hear.

Is there something specific God is asking you to do today? What, if anything, is stopping you from saying yes?

Do you need an Elizabeth in your life? Ask the Lord to show you someone you might approach to act as a mentor in your life. Write down any names that come to mind. Then, like Mary, be bold—ask her!

Do you know someone who could use an Elizabeth? Ask the Lord to bring someone to you. Write down any names that come to mind. Welcome her into your life and speak words of encouragement to her heart.

Eve and Mary were both destined to become life-givers. Each was hand-picked by God to be the mother of all living. The difference between them is not in their capacity. The difference lies in whom they listened to.

Who are you listening to? You have an enemy whose only plan is to destroy you (John 10:10). God wants to give you abundant life. How can you tell the difference?

The place in you that has been dormant can live again. The moment you choose to listen to the truth and run toward a woman who will celebrate your unique destiny, call out your faith, and challenge you to praise God, your tree will grow again.

What would it look like for your tree to grow again? Draw what you see in your journal.

CHAPTER SEVEN

Heroines

HOW TO RECOGNIZE A MODERN-DAY SUPERHERO

• • •

Her children rise up and call her blessed.
Proverbs 31:28, MEV

Powerful women have always been my heroes. Even as a little girl, I had the sneaking suspicion women were supposed to be amazing.

I grew up in the era of *Police Woman*, *Charlie's Angels*, and *Wonder Woman*. They were all crime fighters and female champions. Once, in high school, I was told I looked like Lynda Carter, the original Wonder Woman. I liked that! Not only was she beautiful, but the woman had brains too.

Who wouldn't want to be a superhero? You get a great suit, gorgeous hair, and magic equipment. And you get to help people, even rescue them from life-and-death situations. You have the power to set wrongs right. Good always wins and evil is always overcome.

I still want to be like those amazing heroines. But I know powerful women don't have it so great. Being a woman isn't always cool, and it's almost never easy.

I've come to realize my perception of a superhero is a

myth—an ideal concept of what the perfect woman could be or do.

The birth of my children awakened me to the realization that the true heroines of this world are mothers.

MOTHERS

It has always been God's plan to bless the world through the channel of mothers. After all, 100 percent of the human race has been birthed through a woman! But I'm not just talking about natural birth, although that is at the very core of our purpose. I'm referring to our ability to serve other women, to help them "give birth" to the dreams, plans, and goals God has for them. We can do the same for our husbands and sons. You and I can be a daughter to only one woman, but we can be spiritual mothers to many. This special ability makes us potential heroines.

When God revealed His amazing plan to Mary through the angel, Gabriel immediately told her about Elizabeth. Why? I think it's because he knew she couldn't accomplish this extraordinary task alone. She needed another woman to come alongside her, right from the start. We all need spiritual moms in our lives to help us accomplish everything our heavenly Father has in store for us.

There are many ways to become a mother and numerous opportunities to give life. Let's consider a few.

MENTORS

In this age of high-speed Internet, instant messaging, and the world at our fingertips (literally!), you would think we'd all have more free time to relax and enjoy life. But the opposite seems to be true. The quicker we do things, the more things we find to do, and our days get filled to capacity...and then some.

For centuries women were naturally mentored through their family relationships. Generations lived and worked together. Today we live in single-family units. What we used to learn vicariously, we now have to seek out with intention. We learn to cook through television shows and how-to videos. Much of our child-rearing instruction comes from pop culture. Our education and careers are built through online communities. Social media shapes our relationships. Although this streamlines the process and is in some ways effective, it doesn't leave much room for one-on-one mentoring.

At Gateway Church we have some tremendous programs designed to identify, develop, and connect people for one-on-one ministry and small-group opportunities. Despite the proven effectiveness of these kinds of relationships, and the ever-increasing number of women who are desperately seeking a mentor, we continue to struggle with a shortage of women who will commit to this type of investment.

This shortage is linked not only to a lack of time, but also a lack of confidence. We tend to think we don't have much to offer and that someone younger wouldn't be interested in our life experience or wisdom.

We couldn't be more wrong.

Gateway recently hosted a weekend retreat for ladies ages eighteen to twenty-nine. We brought in approximately forty "older women" to love on them. Here is the response from one of the lovely young women who attended:

You and I can only be a daughter to one woman, but we can be spiritual mothers to many.

As soon as we newbies arrived at the retreat, a group of older women came in whooping, hollering, and clapping to welcome us. Their enthusiasm was obviously genuine, and a great way to start the weekend.

For two very full days those women poured encouragement, wisdom, and vision into our lives. Each session included a relevant message taught by someone who wasn't afraid to speak from personal experience. In a panel session, where any of us could ask whatever questions were on our hearts, they bolstered our faith as they corrected, uplifted, and challenged us. Those women were authentic and open about their lives.

On the last evening, the older women prayed for us. Every young lady there asked for and received prayer. Afterward we all left the retreat dancing (literally!) in the joy of the relationships formed and the insights granted to us.

I came home from the weekend with a few key messages from God about my life, and with the knowledge that there were ladies I could count on to support and mentor me.

Young women today are eagerly seeking the insight, wisdom, and direction of someone more experienced. She doesn't have to be much older—just a few years ahead can make a huge difference.

Another friend of mine shared with me how having a mentor—and then losing her—affected her life:

> As a thirty-year-old I went forward during an altar call and accepted Christ. On my second visit to that church, an older woman sought me out and asked if she could disciple me. She was my first mentor and we greatly enjoyed each other's company.
>
> After a few months, my husband and I relocated to another state. I found a new church home, where I threw myself into serving. I hoped I would find a new mentor and new friends. Over the years, I made several acquaintances but only developed a few real friendships. That mentor relationship never came along again. I continue to feel something is missing.

If you're a twenty-something, there are teen girls who need help navigating their high school years. If you're a thirty-something, there are young professionals and college-age women who want to know how you made the transition from single to married, or from school to work. If you're forty-something, there are women who need to know how to balance jobs, home, and children. They need their marriages built up and their finances set in order. If you are fifty or older, you have a broad range of experience to draw from, and many women want to know how you navigated the challenges of life. They especially need to see how your faith has impacted your journey.

Everyone needs a little help along the way, and everyone has something to offer.

MIDWIVES

The present-day method of childbearing has only been around for a short time. For thousands of years, before modern medicine and birthing suites, mothers delivered babies in their homes with the assistance, guidance, and care of other women in the community. Those who had lots of experience assisting mothers in childbirth became known as midwives.

In Exodus 1 we read about the Hebrew people during the time of their enslavement to the Egyptians. In the midst of their captivity, they became a very fruitful nation. Their numbers grew so rapidly Pharaoh, the ruler of Egypt, became concerned about the threat the Hebrews could pose to his nation if they banded together and aligned themselves with Egypt's enemies.

Desperate to stop the rapid expansion of the Hebrew people, Pharaoh came up with a diabolical plan. He commanded two Hebrew midwives to kill all the male babies they delivered to the Hebrew women.

But those midwives feared God and disobeyed Pharaoh. They let the boys live. Women today desperately need "midwives," women who specialize in assisting other women in birthing not only natural children but also the dreams and destinies of their hearts. Women who will "watch our backs" and refuse to snuff out the life in our dreams.

A good "midwife" does more than provide delivery assistance at the time of "birth." She comes alongside a woman during her "pregnancy," when a dream is planted in her heart, and helps her adjust to the growing capacity within her as she prepares for this major transition. The midwife helps bring dreams to life. She walks alongside a younger woman and encourages her to protect and guard the life within. Then, at the moment of "birth," she aids in managing this most difficult and painful part of the process. Afterward, she not only celebrates the victory but also teaches the woman how to nurture, hold, and care for the dream that has been birthed out of her heart.

Everyone needs a little help along the way, and everyone has something to offer.

The enemy wants to kill the things in our spirits that are designed to bring forth life. We need women who will coach us into choosing life over death. An encouraging wise woman can help another woman avoid aborting her dreams and her destiny in a moment of threat, fear, or panic.

If God has put a dream in you, but the path to accomplishing that goal seems impossible, don't give up hope. Thankfully, our enemy's murderous and cruel plans do not hinder God. He comes right into our places of captivity and shows off His power. The greater our oppression, the more glorious our delivery.

Ask God to send a "midwife" to help you along to your destiny. He will provide someone to encourage you by saying things like, "You can do this. I've been here myself, gotten through it, and seen the outcome of blessing. I know how to navigate in this transition. I'm not letting go until you give birth, and I will help you protect your dreams."

SURROGATE MOTHERS

Today we are more equipped than ever to assist couples in overcoming infertility issues and bearing their own children. Technology and medical interventions are astonishing. Some couples have even gone so far as to utilize a surrogate to assist them in having a baby. A *surrogate* is defined as one who takes the place of another. While this may seem like a modern-day solution, surrogates have been around for ages.

Remember Sarah, Rachel, and Leah? They all called upon their maids to act as surrogates on their behalf. These women, although they may not have chosen it, brought forth life on behalf of those who could not. They were used as life-giving carriers to help others overcome a season of barrenness.

I believe surrogacy is close to the heart of God. Maybe you've never really considered this thought. Christ became a sacrificial substitute—a surrogate—for you and me. Let me explain.

When Christ was on the cross He engaged in the greatest battle ever fought as He willingly bore our sins for us. Despite His own sinlessness, He became a sacrificial substitute for all who would believe. When He fully "labored" under the weight of separation from the Father, He experienced the death that was promised to Adam, Eve, and us. In other words, He did the work, the labor, for us. He became a surrogate for our death.

Thankfully that was not the end of the story.

Three days later He overcame death and arose. As a result of His resurrection, we can now freely receive His gift of eternal life. When we are "born again" we become surrogates, bearing the presence of the Holy Spirit and becoming conduits of His life. We are barren no more.

On the day He arose from the grave, He won not just a battle but the whole war. He overcame death and defeated Satan. He fulfilled the prophecy from Genesis 3 and crushed the head of our enemy. From that moment on, the outcome of our skirmishes was determined. You and I have been restored to our original design, as carriers of God's image, life, and love. We who were bearers of death have divinely become vessels of life.

We need women who will coach us into choosing life over death.

You and I are also in the business of being life-giving surrogates in other ways too. We can partner with our sisters and assist them in sustaining and nurturing their offspring. We can become a secondary carrier of their dreams and destinies. We can pour strength on a struggling mom and blessings on a vulnerable baby. We can also serve young women who are orphaned, literally or figuratively. We can become substitute moms to those who are in broken relationships with their families.

Perhaps you know someone who has a dream in her heart but does not have the skills, abilities, or confidence to fulfill her dream. You could be the answer to this woman's prayers. Your spiritual womb, designed to carry life, may be what's needed to help another carry her dreams to full term.

ADOPTING MOTHERS

Because the midwives in Exodus 1 refused to take the lives of the Hebrew baby boys, our Old Testament deliverer, Moses, survived the mandate of death. His mother and his sister hid him for as long as they could, trying to protect and nurture his life. When they could no longer hide him, they placed him in a basket and set it in the Nile River.

I cannot imagine how desperate Moses's mother must have been to release her infant like that. Perhaps she got the idea from a vision or a dream. The Egyptian slave masters were searching the homes of the Hebrews to find the baby boys. I wonder if his sister, Miriam, is the one who came up with the notion to launch him into the mighty Nile and see what happened.

As Pharaoh's daughter was walking along the river, she noticed a basket among the reeds. When she opened it and saw the baby inside, she felt compassion for him. She knew immediately he was one of the Hebrew infants her father had ordered to be killed. She had to have known the consequences of intervening in this situation, the personal cost to herself and her household. She could have walked away and let the baby die. She could have drowned him. She could have called the Egyptian slave masters and given the baby to them. Yet she did none of those things.

Miriam, who had been hiding in the reeds, did a very

brave thing. She courageously approached Pharaoh's daughter and made what we'd call today an "assumed sale." Assuming the princess would want to save the child's life, she said, "Should I go and find one of the Hebrew women to nurse the baby for you?" (Exod. 2:7).

When the princess agreed, Miriam ran to secure her mother's assistance. Unknowingly, Pharaoh's daughter assigned the child to his own mother and offered to pay her for his care.

God can use us to re-mother those who need nurture, affection, and acceptance.

This woman, moved by kindness, chose to become an adoptive mother to Moses. She was uniquely positioned to come alongside him and preserve his life. She shared with him her resources, her home, and her influence. Moses's birth mother was also uniquely positioned to preserve his life. In order for Moses to fulfill his destiny, she had to allow another woman to mother her child.

God used both of these women to protect Israel's future deliverer by putting him right under the nose of his enemy.

Moses grew up with the influence of two mothers: one natural, one adopted. Both were required to prepare him for his destiny and purpose.

Sometimes we too need many mothers. If we are like Moses, somehow seemingly orphaned by our circumstances, we may need a princess of our own to step in on our behalf. Whether we have mothers, sisters, and families who actually care for us, or if we are instead suffering from an orphan spirit, God will allow another mother to step up at the moment of our need and offer her wisdom, nurture, acceptance, and protection.

Our feminine legacy is now one of love, grace, and eternal life.

You and I can also be mothers to other women. We can open our hearts and homes to those who are emotional orphans. Each of us has the privilege of coming alongside our sisters and, being moved by compassion, offering ourselves as a helper, protector, and provider. We can share from our life-giving storehouse a safe harbor, a word of wise counsel, or even a lifetime relationship. God can use us to re-mother those who need nurture, affection, and acceptance.

You and I have already experienced the unique grace of having been rescued through adoption. Romans 8:15 tells us, "You did not receive the spirit of bondage again to fear, but you received the spirit of adoption by whom we cry out, 'Abba, Father'" (NKJV). We have a heavenly Father who has graciously given us His name, authority, and love. We have a brother in Jesus who willingly laid down His own life to deliver us from death. Our "Daddy" gives us both natural and spiritual families to care for us and help bring about our destinies. He has replaced our generational curses with an abundance of generational blessings. We are now part of a royal family line, with all the privileges and responsibilities of a daughter.

We can serve other women as moms, mentors, midwives, surrogates, and even adopting mothers—life-givers. Those who feel rejected, threatened, or overlooked can be set in families. Those who are vulnerable and unable to care for themselves can be stabilized and nurtured. What was meant by Satan to be a devastating blow in an endless war can become the doorway to life and peace.

STILL A WONDER WOMAN

Now that I'm an adult, married with four kids, I live a seemingly ordinary life. I am swiftly passing my midlife years, watching my children become grown-ups, celebrating thirty-plus years of marriage and daily trying to keep up with the care of my mother. I'm often overwhelmed by my many failings as a wife, a mom, a daughter, and a friend. If I'm not careful, I'll concentrate on my sins, believe the lies of the enemy, and become convinced I am weak and powerless.

But the truth is, somewhere inside me there is still a whisper of a Wonder Woman. I'm guessing that whisper is within you too. After all, when you and I called on the name of Jesus Christ, we instantly became a new creation. In that moment we were adopted into a royal family line. We were wonderfully made in our mothers' wombs, equipped, suited, and empowered by the Holy Spirit to be heroines and to lead people to places of wholeness, love, and victory. Our feminine legacy is now one of love, grace, and eternal life.

. . .

QUESTIONS FOR REFLECTION

I wonder if you have ever thought of yourself as a hero. Maybe I'm the only one with such lofty dreams. Maybe you've been so hurt that you are more prone to think of yourself as a victim. Let's take some time to consider what makes us truly great and how we can more effectively partner with God to reignite our life-giving powers so we can become heroes to others around us. I think you are a wonder woman.

Growing up, who were your heroines? Describe one or two of them.

What about that person made her so appealing?

Who are your heroines now? What makes them appealing?

In chapter 5 we addressed the need to forgive those who may have wounded us, even unintentionally. It's possible your mother fits into this category. If you find you need to begin to walk in forgiveness toward your mother (and there's no shame or dishonor if you do; most of us need to forgive our mothers on some level), take the opportunity now to talk to God about that. If you need to, refer back to the exercise at the end of chapter 5.

Make a list of the positive things your mother contributed to your life. How have those things shaped you or even your own parenting for good?

Take a few moments and celebrate your mom. Make a list of things you are grateful for and consider communicating those to her.

Now make a list of the negative things your mom contributed to your life. How have those things impacted your life?

Have you forgiven your mom (or other women who may have served you in a similar capacity) for how she may have hurt you? How will forgiving these women change the way you live?

Who are some other women who may have mothered you? List their qualities.

Is there someone in your life who might need mothering? Who might need someone to come alongside her and nurture, encourage, and protect her? Consider being something of an adoptive mother to her. Commit to take the risk and reach out!

Women today desperately need "midwives," women who specialize in assisting other women in birthing not only natural children, but also the dreams and destinies of their hearts.

What does the description of a midwife birth in your heart? Do you recognize your own need for someone to act as a midwife for your dreams and destiny? Ask God to lead you to a woman who can commit to helping you birth those things in your heart.

Perhaps you are called to walk alongside another woman, to support her in her own process. What experiences have you had that might encourage someone else?

CHAPTER EIGHT

Called to the Front Lines

WOMEN HAVE THE POWER TO MULTIPLY

• • •

Before I formed you in the womb I knew you;
and before you were born I sanctified you, and
I ordained you a prophet to the nations.

Jeremiah 1:5, MEV

Early in my pastoring days I had a significant encounter with God over the matter of women. I was serving as a pastor in a small church, and I put together a plan for a group of us to travel out of town and attend another church's retreat. We divided up among four vehicles to make the trip. Naturally, we broke up by relationship and life status. I drove the lead car, and our young women were in the car at the end of the caravan.

We hadn't been on the road very long when I began to sense their resistance to follow my lead. They drove their own speed and made their own stops. I was constantly checking my rearview mirror, slowing down for them, or making U-turns to go back and get them. This was only a slight annoyance, but it became a definite frustration for me.

When we arrived at the meeting facility, we again divided up by friends, so the young ladies separated from the majority of the group. I had assumed they would want to hang out with the rest of us and enjoy the opportunity to experience together a "retreat within a retreat." Several things they said and did let me know that wasn't going to happen.

Being a young leader and not really understanding the dynamics of the situation, I became upset. Since I had certain expectations about how they should behave (which I had not bothered to communicate to them), I felt personally rejected and disrespected. I hid my thoughts from the ladies around me, but not from the Lord.

That evening during the ministry time, I got on my face before God, asking Him to help me deal with my feelings.

Suddenly I felt a tap on my shoulder. One of the young ladies sank down next to me. She apologized for her behavior and told me she had a hard time with women. I realized she'd resisted my leadership because she felt I was trying to "mother" her.

**Often we lack the power to multiply
what God has given us because we are
too busy focusing on what we lack.**

My heart broke. All my frustration melted away and I was filled with compassion. We prayed together and forgave each other. The rest of the weekend moved forward with much greater unity.

The next afternoon, I was alone in my room, thanking God for the breakthrough, when the Lord distinctly told me, "You are a mother to mothers."

He named me.

It was similar to when He changed Simon's name to Peter or Saul to Paul or Sarai to Sarah. He breathed on me in that moment and I was marked. I have never been the same. I guess you could say I received special marching orders that day. In a moment I was activated for service and called to the front lines of the battle.

I've sometimes wrestled with this idea, and many times I have failed miserably to live up to the assignment. But it was deposited in me like a seed, and it has been growing more fruitful ever since. It is not something I can develop on my own. It is my calling, and it grows as I yield myself more to its purpose and power.

The encounter with that young lady was my first example of a moment where I could step into another woman's life and serve her as a mother. In her moment of vulnerability, God graced me to respond with nurture, comfort, and love. It sprang forth from the place in me that was being healed.

A CHAIN REACTION

When God named me, He set in motion a sequence of events that established a foundation upon which I could begin to build a legacy of love for the women in my life. In a manner of speaking, He activated what was great in me: my ability to give life.

All of us have received a name and a call. The Commander-in-Chief of the angel armies has dispatched His Son to lead us into victory. You and I have been invited to report to duty. He is waiting for us to come front and center in order to receive our assignments.

Scripture tells us:

> Your job is to speak out on the things that make for solid doctrine.... Guide older women into lives of reverence so they end up as neither gossips nor drunks, but models of goodness. By looking at them, the younger women will know how to love their husbands and children, be virtuous and pure, keep a good house, be good wives.... Mostly, show them all this by doing it yourself, incorruptible in your teaching, your words solid and sane. Then anyone who is dead set against us, when he finds nothing weird or misguided, might eventually come around.
> —Titus 2:1–8, THE MESSAGE

If the world were perfect, we would be born, grow up, give birth, grow old, become grandmothers (mothers to mothers), and enter our eternal destiny happy with our lives. Our legacy would be that our daughters experience the same cycle of grace. We would be caught up in a chain reaction of Titus 2 proportions.

You and I have been given a mandate to lead younger women into lives of righteousness. However, their "chain reactions" are often broken. Many women are born into cycles and situations that are in exact opposition to God's perfect plan. We can no longer hang back in the battle for their destinies. We have been assigned to make disciples who are strong, whole, and clear about their calling.

POWER TO MULTIPLY

God's intention has always been for humankind to be fruitful and multiply abundantly. As a result, we have the power to multiply everything He gives us.

All of us have received a name and a call.

When two become one, there is the power of multiplication. This is true with a male and female in marriage, but it is also true in every other relationship. When two women draw together and create a godly rapport—mother to daughter, sister to sister, or friend to friend—there is an innate potential to produce life, to impart love, and to multiply a blessing.

So why don't we see more multiplication in our lives? Often we lack the power to multiply what God has given us because we are too busy focusing on what we lack. Rather than asking ourselves, "What do I have?" we talk to God about what we don't have. More than that, we focus on our failures and our wounds, believing lies that produce death, and spend our lives unaware of the potential that lies within us.

Most of us don't give thanks to God in our places of lack. We look at our limited resources or our finite time and we complain or worry. We consider our brokenness to have no value.

What would happen if we just blessed those things?

I don't mean we have to be grateful for curses like cancer. But I do appreciate that cancer, which tried to destroy me, ushered in a new beginning for me, where God showed me His faithfulness in magnificent ways. We don't have to give thanks for abuse. But we can be grateful abuse gives us the ability to recognize true love and acceptance and to know what a miracle it is to experience healing. You wouldn't naturally give thanks for death. But we can appreciate that the loss of our natural life can be a doorway to eternal life, where we will never again experience pain, grief, or lack.

Jesus showed us the key to multiplication. Do you remember when He fed the multitude with a few fish and loaves of bread? (Read more about this in Matthew 14, Mark 6, Luke 9, and John 6.) It wasn't until He broke and blessed what the disciples said was not enough. Even out of imperfect starts, dormant wombs, and relational devastation, many women have become wonderful life-givers.

Now consider what would have happened if the little boy who had the few fish and loaves of bread had refused to give it to Jesus. Thousands of people would have gone hungry—not just the one boy, who didn't really have enough anyway.

Most of us are afraid to give the little we have to another. When we feel we don't have enough of something, we tend to hoard it, fearful we won't have what we need. This causes us to be stingy. And God won't multiply what we don't offer. Sometimes what we have to offer is the place of our barrenness or lack. Our pain and loss seem insufficient as an offering to Christ. Yet when you bless what you previously called cursed, you position yourself for a miracle of mathematical proportions.

Why not give Christ the "little" you have? It's not sufficient to sustain you anyway. Go ahead and bless the places of your brokenness: your pain, your lack, and your fears. Your successes, your victories, your provision, and your resources won't take you to the places you hope to go either. You must offer what you have to Christ in order to receive a miracle of multiplication.

Be appreciative for everything you have, whether large or small, and be generous with it. Offer it all to Jesus with thankfulness. Generosity times gratitude equals multiplication. If you give what little you have, God will multiply it, and all of us will be able to eat out of the overflow.

It seems God doesn't often multiply us out of our strength or our abundance. Rather, He touches the places inside us that are fragile, shattered, or broken, and in those very places He begins to multiply. What you thought disqualified you is really the thing that qualifies you. What the enemy meant to destroy your destiny is, in fact, the doorway to your fruitfulness.

BECOMING A LIFE-GIVER

My husband and I had been married for five years when we made the decision to have a baby. Neither of us had been quick to take on this responsibility, and I can still remember the weight of the decision. It's one thing to be married and get a little surprise: "Oops! Guess we're going to have a baby!" But it's another thing to consciously choose to bring forth life.

When we did decide to take this journey, we found ourselves unable to conceive. After two years and some medical intervention, I finally became pregnant. I couldn't have been more excited when the doctor confirmed my condition. In the two-year process of trying to have a baby, I had grown deeply in my desire to have a child. This was no longer a mental decision about taking on the responsibility of parenthood. I actually longed to be a mother.

At about six weeks I had some complications that almost resulted in a miscarriage. I prayed fervently for the life of my child to be sustained. Any lingering doubts I may have had about bringing a new life into the world completely dissolved. I was absolutely certain I wanted this baby. I ached to be a mother.

In September of 1990 I finally gave birth to a baby girl. Ashley arrived ten days early, with a few complications. The doctor had to perform a C-section. Everything ended up working out fine, but in the moment of delivery my newborn and I didn't have a chance to bond. The nurse took her from me and I was sent to recovery. Later in the afternoon, when I was finally in my own room (and in my right mind), the nurse brought Ashley to me.

Sometimes the things we birth come only through great battle and perseverance.

As I took her into my arms, I saw how tiny she was—and how beautiful. As I carefully unwrapped the blanket, inspecting her limbs and counting her fingers and toes, my heart exploded with what I can only describe as the sweetest pain I have ever known. A deep, soul-shattering release of love washed over me. I had experienced the love of my parents, my husband, and other people. But I had never known a love like this. I finally understood what life is all about.

I had become a mother. More than that, I became aware of my purpose. In that moment I realized I was made to give life.

OTHER MOTHERS

It doesn't really matter the circumstances or situations into which you were born or even if you have given birth. What matters is what you do with your life-giving experiences. Even out of imperfect starts, dormant wombs, and relational devastation, many women have become wonderful life-givers.

Let's look at a few women from the Bible who overcame some significant obstacles to become life-givers. I'll bet you'll find some moms you can relate to.

Bathsheba

Bathsheba had an extramarital affair with King David that resulted in the birth of a son. Their illicit union set off a whole series of events—and sin—that extended to murder and deception, and the death of the child. To say the beginning of their relationship was out of order would be an understatement.

Yet King David eventually repented of his sin, and another son was born from their union. Solomon turned out to be a peaceable ruler whose wisdom was legendary.

Bathsheba's story can give us hope. Conception is not an indicator of our destiny. Even if you were conceived out of trauma or sin, or if you gave birth in the midst of deception or threat, God has a plan for you and your children. Isaiah 49:1 tells us that before we were born the Lord called us; from our mother's womb He has spoken our names. No matter the circumstances of your birth, you are known and were chosen by God. And even if your children got a rough start, God has His hand upon them. Who knows? The child who was conceived in difficulty might just become a wise ruler or a blessing to the nations.

Hannah

Hannah's story is one of the most poignant in the entire Bible. Like many women, she suffered from barrenness. And, like Leah, she was badly mistreated by her husband's other wife, an extremely fertile woman named Peninnah. In 1 Samuel 1:7 we read, "Her rival wife taunted her cruelly, rubbing it in and never letting her forget that GOD had not given her children. This went on year after year" (THE MESSAGE). Can't you just feel her heartache?

But Hannah didn't wallow in her misery and complain about her circumstances. Nor did she treat Peninnah the way she was being treated. She turned her attention to God and handed her desires over to Him. Rather than allowing bitterness to spring up or return insult for insult, she continually made her requests known to God. Eventually, she gave birth to a son, Samuel, and selflessly devoted him to the service of God's house.

Hannah had five other children. And Samuel became one of the greatest religious and political leaders of his generation, eventually becoming a prophet, priest, and advisor to the kings of Israel.

What would have happened if Hannah had given up under the onslaught of hate and the pain of barrenness? She would have brought misery to herself and her family all of their days. God could not have rewarded her trust in Him by giving her Samuel and her other children. Without Samuel, the kings of Israel would not have received the godly counsel he provided. And we wouldn't know the story of a young bride who overcame her circumstances and believed God for miracles.

God sees, and He can protect, defend, comfort, deliver, and heal you.

Sometimes the things we birth come only through great battle and perseverance. Perhaps you've been persecuted by another woman, or feel as if someone you care about—or God—has overlooked you. Even if you've chosen to duke it out with your enemy in the past, you can choose now to be like Hannah and turn to God with your pain and your needs.

Refuse to waste your strength on bitterness or

unnecessary fights. Rather, consider what you might someday carry in the womb of your spirit and how God could use it for His purposes. Jeremiah 29:11 says, "I know the thoughts that I think toward you, says the LORD, thoughts of peace and not of evil, to give you a future and a hope" (NKJV).

Sarah

Remember Sarah, the one who was so mean to Hagar? Well I have good news! Not only did she overcome her insecurities and her sin, she actually became a mother to nations (Gen. 17:16) when she experienced the fulfillment of the prophetic promise to Abraham through her own body, finally giving birth to Isaac. She and Abraham shared a destiny and a call. The fulfillment of God's promises to Abraham required Sarah's partnership. After all, without Sarah there would be no Isaac.

It's interesting to me that God sent the prophet to a woman who was experiencing tremendous lack in her life—a single mom, just trying to make ends meet.

Perhaps you have taunted, abandoned, or wounded someone else. Maybe you've given up on your dreams and abdicated your righteous position to another. Possibly you've looked at your barrenness and given up on the potential fruitfulness of your marriage, or perhaps even your life. But if you trust God, it's never too late for situations that seem impossible to become possible.

Hagar

Do you know what happened to Hagar? When she escaped from Sarah, she ran straight into the arms of the angel of the Lord. God heard the cries of her heart and sought her out. She called him "the God who sees me." Strengthened by this visit from the Almighty, Hagar returned home, overcame her abuse, and became a mother to Ishmael. And despite the sordid details of his conception, God gave him a divine blessing and an eternal destiny.

Women who are trapped in abusive situations often struggle with their perceptions about God. They cannot comprehend that a loving God would allow something so damaging to happen to them and to their loved ones. They wonder if He really knows what's going on behind closed doors. Or if He actually cares.

The truth is, God does care. Deeply. Abuse is never, ever His will.

Abuse can take all kinds of forms and exist in a variety of relationships. Maybe, like Hagar, you've been emotionally or spiritually rejected. Perhaps you've been physically beaten, or you've suffered verbal assaults. It might not have been a woman who wounded you, but a man. You may have even abused someone yourself.

Don't respond to your pain by shutting other people out. Do some research and find resources that could provide deliverance. Reach out to someone and let him or her know you need help. Consider contacting a friend, a family member, or a local church. Or call an abuse-victim advocacy center or a domestic violence hotline.

Abuse is a crime. If your health, well-being, or life is

threatened, do not hesitate to get out of harm's way. Reach out for help. Then do whatever is necessary to protect yourself and your children.

Whatever else you do, call on the Lord and ask Him to direct your steps. This is not a platitude or a last-ditch effort. God sees, and He can protect, defend, comfort, deliver, and heal you.

Deborah

In the Book of Judges we read about a woman named Deborah. Scripture doesn't mention if she had any children, but it does say she was a wife, a prophet, and a judge over Israel at a time when the nation was in great trouble. "Public roads were abandoned, travelers went by back roads. Warriors became fat and sloppy, no fight left in them" (Judg. 5:6, THE MESSAGE). Deborah lived in a season of political, social, and economic unrest. The leaders of the day had grown lazy and were unwilling to do whatever was required to guard, protect, and build up the country. Sound familiar?

All women are extraordinary—including you.

Deborah refused to allow her nation to go on in such distress. Judges 5:7 says, "I, Deborah, arose…like a mother in Israel" (MEV). Deborah was a working woman who led an entire nation out of bondage and into victory, all from the mantle of motherhood. She did not take on the role of chief warrior or try to subvert the position of the others in her community to accomplish her goals. She simply took the authority that was on her life and the compassion in her heart and invited others to overcome with her.

Those who work outside their homes sometimes find themselves questioning their parenting priorities and worry endlessly about their choices. I've been a working mom most of my married life. I spent a lot of time feeling guilty about pretty much everything. If I was at work, I felt like I should be home. If I was at home, I was often thinking about work. I allowed the enemy to convince me I was a poor mother and a selfish person for contributing to the finances of our home.

Whether you have a job outside the home or not, you work. All mothers do. So embrace your work and do it as unto the Lord. Remain physically available and emotionally attached for your family. Practice being present in every moment. Focus your attention on the matter at hand.

God knows the needs of your family. If you're a stay-at-home mom, great! If you're a working mom, great! If you are a little of both, that's great too. Embrace wherever you are.

The Widow at Zarephath

In 1 Kings 17, we read about an amazing widow—a single mom. Although Scripture does not tell us her name, she is a model of motherhood.

This woman was at the end of her rope. She faced lack in many areas of her life. She had no husband, no provision, and no hope. She and her son were on the verge of starvation. When we encounter her in Scripture, we find her desperately trying to use the little she had to sustain her family for as long as she could.

As she was about to prepare a final meal for herself and her son with the tiny bit of food they had left, God sent the prophet Elijah to her.

Israel was in a severe drought. But God had a plan to meet His prophet's needs as well as the widow's and her son's. He instructed Elijah to travel to Zarephath. "I have commanded a widow there to provide for you" (1 Kings 17:9, MEV). Upon his arrival at the city gate, he saw a woman gathering sticks for a fire and asked her for a bite of bread and a cup of water.

After she explained her dire situation, Elijah encouraged her to risk using up the little she had to feed him. The prophet assured her that if she did, what she had would not run out.

This woman was obedient, daring, or desperate. She did as Elijah requested, and sure enough, her provision did not run out. As a matter of fact, it multiplied enough to feed her, Elijah, and her son for several days. What she thought was the end of her life instead became the doorway to hope.

It's interesting to me that God sent the prophet to a woman who was experiencing tremendous lack in her life—a single mom, just trying to make ends meet.

Single motherhood is a rewarding but difficult journey. Yet women in this situation can be and often are great moms. Some of the best moms I know are single parents. Singleness doesn't have to be a place of lack; Scripture promises that God will be a "father to the fatherless" and a "defender of widows" (Ps. 68:5). One parent plus God is sufficient to form a whole and healthy family.

MODERN-DAY MOMS

While it's great to look at some of the amazing mothers from Scripture, we don't want to overlook the moms of today who are doing an incredible job of overcoming hardships and raising the next generation. My friend Suzette shares a testimony of how her mom is making a difference in her family.

> My mother is a beautiful example of a godly woman. I am overwhelmed with gratefulness to God for her. She has given me unconditional love and encouragement throughout my life. Her prayers and guidance allowed me to know Jesus Christ as my personal Lord and Savior.
>
> My mother is my best friend. I can tell her anything, and she loves me anyway. She is also my prayer warrior. When we pray together, God always answers, and He's done many miracles in our lives.
>
> Mom is my mentor too—my go-to person for advice. Her godly example as a wife and mother has meant the world to me. Only God could put all that wonderful into one person!
>
> I pray I can have this kind of relationship with my daughter as she grows into womanhood. And that I will be able to effectively lead her to look to God to meet her needs and heal her wounds.

GREATNESS

All women are extraordinary—including you. You probably wouldn't call yourself "extraordinary." After all, it doesn't sound very humble. So instead you settle for "good enough." Since you're not a bad person, you think of yourself as a good person.

But God doesn't want us to just be good. We are designed to be great in His eyes. I'm not talking about greatness according to the world's definition, but the kind that comes when you know the Great One. We exist for His glory, and nothing is greater than that. This is why your call to the front lines is so critical. This is why you must come front-and-center to report for duty—because you were created, equipped, and empowered to be a life-giver, graced with the ability to multiply, and you are full of greatness.

· · ·

QUESTIONS FOR REFLECTION

Ready to report for duty? I sure hope so. I love the stories of the women of the Bible. I'm continually amazed at how similar they are to the women in my life. I can always find something about their story that impacts me in a positive manner. You and I are not alone. All of us are on a journey to getting into greater agreement with God's plan. Let's begin this reflection time considering how every season of our life is an opportunity to bless another. Grab your journal and let's get started.

Describe a "birth" in your life, whether physical or spiritual.

Did this birth make you aware of your sense of mothering? What were the circumstances surrounding that event? What was the process like?

You may have begun to feel the stir of new things inside you, becoming expectant of what God might be doing. Stop and list those things and share some of those with a friend. Then ask the Lord to confirm them to you in the next few weeks. Keep track of the confirmations and/or the adjustments in what you are sensing.

God doesn't multiply us out of our strength or our abundance. Rather, He touches the places inside us that are fragile, shattered, or broken, and in those very places He begins to multiply. What you thought disqualified you is really the thing that qualifies you. What the enemy meant to destroy your destiny is in fact the doorway to your fruitfulness.

What are the things you think disqualify you?

If this statement is true, then restate your disqualifications as qualifications. Is there anything here that surprises you?

Now ask God to show you how He can multiply the thing you thought was a disqualification. Journal what you see and hear.

Most of us don't give thanks to God in our places of lack…what would happen if we just gave thanks for these things?

In what areas do you sense "lack"? Are there some places where you just don't have enough? These could be physical, emotional, or spiritual. Write down your concerns.

Like the little boy, take those things and offer them to Jesus. Allow Him to break and bless those things that seem inadequate for your need. Thank Him in advance for the fact that He can bring abundance where we only see lack. Journal your thoughts.

Each of the women discussed in this chapter had a significant challenge to overcome. And each one overcame her challenge in a unique way.

Which of the women discussed here do you most identify with? Why?

What about her life and her ultimate blessing might encourage you as you overcome your own challenges?

Because you were created, equipped, and empowered to be a life-giver, graced with the ability to multiply, you are full of greatness. I'm not talking about greatness as the world would define it, but the kind that comes when you know the Great One.

Declare these words over your life. "I am full of greatness because I know the Great One." There is power in your declaration! (See Proverbs 18:21.)

Ask God to speak to you about the greatness within you. He knows it well; after all, He's the one who put it there! Journal what He tells you.

**In this chapter, we discussed abuse. Abuse is a crime. If your (or your children's) health, well-being, or life is threatened, do not hesitate to get out of harm's way. Reach out for help. Contact the National Domestic Violence Hotline at 1-800-799-SAFE (7233) or for more information, go to www.thehotline.org. God desires that you and your family would be safe!

CHAPTER NINE

The Most Powerful Weapon

LAYING DOWN YOUR LIFE FOR ANOTHER

. . .

This is My commandment: that you love one another,
as I have loved you. Greater love has no man than
this: that a man lay down his life for his friends.
John 15:12–13, MEV

I want to walk in power—godly power. I like to watch God show up in ways I can see and hear and feel. So I've spent a lot of time and effort increasing my knowledge and understanding about things related to the power of God. I've been in the presence of people who move in power. I've been touched by power. On occasion, I've even been able to pray with power. However, my ability to walk a consistent life of power has been less than noteworthy.

In 2006 my husband and I made a major life transition. We moved from a small community in West Texas to the heart of the Dallas/Fort Worth area. At the time, I felt confused about the purpose for this change and asked

God what it was all about. He told me the coming year was going to be about love.

To be honest, I felt a little disappointed. I wanted to talk with God about more power. (Please tell me I'm not the only one!)

THE FRUIT OF THE SPIRIT

At a conference I attended a few years ago, in the midst of the speaker's presentation, I was interrupted by a thought saying, *"My power flows on the fruit of the Spirit."*

Wanting to hear what the speaker was saying, I jotted down the words and tried to focus, but I couldn't get that sentence out of my mind.

Over the next several months, I spent a good deal of time contemplating the fruit of the Spirit: love, joy, peace, patience, kindness, goodness, faithfulness, gentleness, and self-control (Gal. 5:22). Every time I heard something about love or joy or peace, I was reminded of the words I heard at the conference.

As I studied the fruit of the Spirit, I realized cultivating spiritual fruit takes the emphasis off me and puts the focus on others. It creates an atmosphere where there is potential for God to move in power. I become less and He becomes greater. The simplest acts of kindness can help others to see further, hope more, and listen better.

I want to walk in power—godly power.

Then I thought about the similarities between spiritual fruit and earthly fruit. Fruit is cultivated, grows from seed, can be easily damaged or destroyed, and must be reproduced season after season. It is perishable and meant for quick consumption. It is sweet and beautiful and multicolored. It requires a long season of cultivation and many seasons of pruning to produce a mighty harvest. When it finally reaches maturity, it is ripe, rich and flowing, ready to be given away freely. Most exciting of all, fruit carries within itself the power to reproduce—the very seeds of life.

I gradually switched from begging God for power and instead started seeking fruit. This pattern of prayer became like a trail that led me down a path and then onto a road. Eventually, I began to see a "highway of love" up ahead. A highway is a large, cross-country, multi-lane, multi-access road to get a lot of people where they want to go as quickly, easily, and safely as possible. It is designed to deliver them to a particular destination, overcoming all kinds of obstacles and roadblocks along the way. Even the term "highway" carries the connotation of choosing a better path.

If I focus more on God's power than on the fruit of the Spirit, I end up traveling in circles, missing the access ramp to the destination I've been dreaming about. But when I let go of my need to be the deliverer of power, I become a highway of love upon which God's presence and power can move.

No wonder whenever I ask God for more power, He responds by asking me for more fruit.

THE GIFTS OF THE SPIRIT

In 1 Corinthians 12, we read about the gifts of the Spirit, which include wisdom, knowledge, faith, healings, the working of miracles, prophecy, discerning of spirits, different kinds of tongues, and interpretation of tongues (vv. 8–11). In chapters 12 and 14, we learn about the operation of these gifts.

Chapter 12 ends with, "I will show you the most excellent way" (v. 31, NIV). Chapter 14 begins with, "Follow the way of love" (v. 1, NIV). It's kind of like chapter 13 (often called "the love chapter") is the creamy white stuff of an Oreo cookie. You can take a nice big bite and eat the whole cookie (chapters 12, 13, and 14) all at once, or you can break apart those cookie containers and relish the inside first.

Chapter 13 includes a focused description of the greatest fruit of all: love.

> Love is patient, love is kind. It does not envy, it does not boast, it is not proud. It is not rude, it is not self-seeking, it is not easily angered, it keeps no record of wrongs. Love does not delight in evil but rejoices with the truth. It always protects, always trusts, always hopes, always perseveres. Love never fails.
>
> —1 Corinthians 13:4–7, NIV

THE GREATEST OF THESE

First Corinthians 13:13 tells us when all is said and done, three things remain: faith, hope, and love. "But the greatest of these is love" (MEV).

All of the spiritual gifts are good and have purpose, but

love is the most powerful tool we have to transform the human heart and impact generations.

Love is a universal language. It bypasses every cultural barrier, racial difference, language challenge, and religious persuasion. It is far greater than any talent, skill, or assignment you can have. Love will move mountains. Love will mend hearts. Love will transform. It will override every form of bondage, overcome every rejection, and heal every wound.

Whenever we stumble upon hate, we know Satan is at work. Anything in your life that is marred by hate, or has been stolen, killed, or destroyed, is evidence of the work of our enemy. If there is a deep wound in your life, it doesn't mean there's something inherently wrong with you. There is something inherently wrong with him. What's in you is exactly the opposite of what's in the enemy. He hates. You love.

LOVE OVERCOMES

If we want to break the cycle of wounding, self-sabotage, and injury to one another, you and I are going to have to learn how to be fruitful and give love.

Let me share with you a story from the Bible about a bitter woman who discovered the power of God's love, which enabled her to overcome her pain, disappointment, and bitterness. As a result, she was able to love others and she was abundantly blessed. The story starts with this woman's daughter-in-law.

Ruth loved her husband despite the differences in their upbringing. Life with his extended family had its challenges.

Yet there was something about their family, and especially her mother-in-law, Naomi, that spoke to Ruth.

Ruth and Naomi were very different from one another. They came from different cultures and spiritual backgrounds. They were in different age brackets. They had different family histories. They had different native languages. These two women were different in every way you can imagine.

When Ruth's husband, father-in-law, and brother-in-law all died, she must have wondered what would happen to her. Living in a home filled with grief and a mother-in-law who was so devastated she even called herself "bitter" (Ruth 1:20) couldn't have been easy.

These are the kinds of women I want to pattern my life after, ones who allow love to overcome bitterness.

In the depths of their grief, Naomi announced that she was returning to her hometown. Both of her daughters-in-law chose to follow her. Not long after starting out on the difficult and dangerous journey, Naomi urged them to go back to their homes and families, lamenting her obvious inability to meet their needs. One daughter-in-law, despite her protests and tears, turned back. But not Ruth.

In one of the most beautiful passages of Scripture, Ruth declared her passion for Naomi's God and her love for her mother-in-law. She said, "Don't force me to leave you; don't make me go home. Where you go, I go; and where you live, I'll live. Your people are my people, your God is my god; where you die, I'll die, and that's where I'll be buried, so help me GOD—not even death itself is going to come between us!" (Ruth 1:16–17, THE MESSAGE).

In this moment Ruth made a critical choice. It was about more than turning back. She had to decide whether or not to become bitter about her circumstances. She could have turned away from Naomi, losing the last and final connection of her marriage. Instead she chose to press on, declaring her loyalty. Ruth chose to tie her life to her mother-in-law's life and walk on together. As it turned out, this was a very wise decision; as a result, she was richly blessed. She overcame her loss and created a family.

Out of this commitment Ruth was adopted into the Hebrew clan. She received a redeemer who not only restored abandoned land and reclaimed an inheritance that was lost, but he also received her as his bride. She also bore a son of promise, who became part of Jesus's family tree.

And what about Naomi? When she lost her husband and her sons, she felt abandoned by God. She became bitter and angry. Yet when Ruth declared her intentions, Naomi embraced God's purposes and became a mentor and a mother to Ruth. In the process Naomi got a new home, new friends, a son-in-law, a grandson, and a heart of gratitude.

These are the kinds of women I want to pattern my life after, ones who allow love to overcome bitterness. This is the kind of response I want to be able to give when someone tries to turn me away or when I notice a woman trapped in pain…even if it's me who's trapped. This is the kind of fruit I want to see in my life.

GOD IS LOVE

All you need is love. The Beatles captured the essence of the pop culture of the sixties with their impactful song about the "love generation." Those words make love sound so simple. But in the day-to-day crucible of life, it can be difficult—even seemingly impossible—to love some people, especially those who've wounded us.

Sometimes it's not even easy to love ourselves.

Life isn't perfect. None of us are perfect. If we could go back to the Garden of Eden we would, but we can't. In an attempt to soothe our wounds and recreate perfection, we put our focus on lots of external things such as achievements, our appearance, membership in the right groups, even plastic surgery. But none of it can really help heal these kinds of wounds. When we've been hurt, the natural response isn't love, but hate. Even if we turn the offenses of others over to God and allow Him to uproot the hatred in our hearts, it doesn't mean we will automatically feel love for those who have hurt us.

When we realize God is love, that catchy phrase begins to make sense. All you really need is God. He loves you with an infinite, unconditional love. And He can fill you with a love for others that goes far beyond anything you could try to manufacture in yourself. He enables us to love the unlovable.

Love is the most powerful tool we have to transform the human heart and impact generations.

John 3:16 says, "For God so loved the world that He gave His only begotten Son" (MEV). You could say, "Love so loved!" Only God, through the gift of His Son and by the work of the Holy Spirit, can deposit love into our hearts. You and I can't "make" love—we can only receive it.

If you don't know God as a friend, perhaps it's because you've never accepted Jesus as your Savior. You can't know this love we've been discussing if you don't know God is love. If you need more love you simply need to know God more fully.

Revelation 3:20 says, "Listen! I stand at the door and knock. If anyone hears My voice and opens the door, I will come in and dine with him, and he with Me" (MEV). And Romans 10:9 says, "If you confess with your mouth Jesus is Lord, and believe in your heart that God has raised Him from the dead, you will be saved" (MEV).

If you've never invited Jesus to save you, may I encourage you to ask Him to come into your life right now? If you're not sure what to say, you can pray something like this:

God, I need Your forgiveness and Your love. I believe Jesus Christ died for my sins and He was raised from the dead. Right now I want Jesus to become my Lord and Savior. Fill me with Your Spirit. Thank You for Your mercy and grace. Thank You for eternal life. Help me to bring glory and honor to You in everything I do.

And Lord, teach me to love.

If you said that prayer, you have just entered into a relationship that is profound and life-changing. Accepting

Jesus as your Lord and Savior is just the beginning. As you come to know God more, the love of Christ in you will begin to transform your life. You can begin to experience the fullness of God's grace. And if you need more love than you currently possess, you only have to ask Him for it. Prayer will jump-start a surge of love in your heart for God and for His people. More love than you ever imagined can flood your soul.

When you are filled with God's love on a daily basis, that love will eventually swell up and overflow onto others. Your family. Your friends. Your coworkers. People you used to think of as enemies. Even strangers. You'll have compassion for those in pain because you have a surplus of love.

The truth is, you can't love if you don't know love.

When we read about Jesus in the Gospels, we see He did everything out of love. We are told Jesus "had compassion" or was "moved with compassion" before He miraculously healed the sick (Matt. 14:14), fed the hungry (Matt. 15:32), gave sight to the blind (Matt. 20:34), cleansed the unclean (Mark 1:41), prevented death from a distance (Mark 5:19), and taught the multitude about the heavenly Father (Mark 7:34). His heart of love preceded His miracles.

Jesus allowed love to become a highway on which His power flowed. We too can see miracles, signs, and wonders if we follow the pattern of Christ, starting with love.

All the time I spent and the effort I exerted trying to get more God-power into my life was misdirected. I realize now that I should have been pursuing more love. More compassion. More grace and forgiveness toward the people in my life, even those who have hurt me. Even toward myself. If I can love people the way Jesus did, I will have the power within me to lead them to miracles of restoration and healing.

• • •

QUESTIONS FOR REFLECTION

This chapter is truly full of the "good news" that God is love. I'm praying for you as you turn your focus from wounds and loss to love and overcoming. Whether you realize it or not, you are developing your testimony. A testimony comes only after the test! Love washing over your life will produce a beautiful faith that is vibrant and full of the fruit of the Spirit. I am proud of you for persevering on this journey and for being willing to discover the truth in the Beatles song "All You Need Is Love."

Describe your favorite fruit. Use colorful words: juicy, sweet, etc.

Commit Galatians 5:22–23 to memory. "But the Holy Spirit produces this kind of fruit in our lives: love, joy, peace, patience, kindness, goodness, faithfulness, gentleness and self-control…"

Consider the fruit of the Spirit in your own life. Which fruit are you successfully demonstrating and how? Which fruit would you like to see become more abundant? Ask God for greater fruitfulness and write down what you hear in your journal.

The Word of God is "living and active" (Heb. 4:12) and creative (Gen. 1, Ps. 33:6). As we meditate on it we are not just thinking of words; we're actually activating something powerful and transforming in our lives. As you work through this section, journal your experience.

What is the difference between "fruit" and "gifts" as described in this chapter?

Define "love" in your own terms.

Describe how love affected Ruth's life. What choices did she make as a result of her love for Naomi?

Describe how love affected Naomi. How did her love for Ruth affect her "bitter" heart?

First John 4:8 tells us *God is love.*

How does that statement make you feel?

> Love is patient, love is kind. It does not envy, it does not boast, it is not proud. It is not rude, it is not self-seeking, it is not easily angered, it keeps

no record of wrongs. Love does not delight in evil but rejoices with the truth. It always protects, always trusts, always hopes, always perseveres. Love never fails.

—1 Corinthians 13:4–7, NIV

Read your earlier definition of "love" and compare it to the passage from 1 Corinthians. How do the two match up?

The word for "repent" in the Bible is the Greek word *metanoeo*, which literally means to "change your mind" or "change your thinking." This doesn't mean simply introducing a new thought; it means a whole new way of thinking, a whole new way of seeing. God asks us to "repent" from our old ways of thinking and "renew our minds" (Rom. 12:2), bringing our thoughts into alignment with His.

Perhaps you need to "repent" of your definition of love and allow Him to introduce a whole new way of viewing it. If so, let this prayer serve as a guide.

God, I repent. I give up my definition of love and ask You to give me Yours. I ask You to heal those places where my thinking may be less than Your best, where I may have wounds that have caused me to reject love as You define it.

Would You show me how You love me? Thank You, Lord, for loving me!

Let Him show you how He loves you and add His answer to your journal!

CHAPTER TEN

One Good Soldier

It All Begins with You

. . .

Endure hard times as a good soldier of Jesus Christ. No soldier on active duty entangles himself with civilian affairs, that he may please the enlisting officer.
2 Timothy 2:3–4, MEV

I am extremely blessed to have a lot of great girlfriends. But that hasn't always been the case. For most of my life, my soul was too influenced by culture, wounded by circumstance, and calloused by selfishness to see the incredible women around me.

Since I had no brothers or sisters, everything I learned early on about peer relationships developed in a school setting. As a teenager, I ran with a group of girls who competed for the attention of boys, stabbed one another in the back, and walked away when a friendship was inconvenient. I'm sure I was the leader of the pack. I didn't hate girls—I just didn't know them, and I certainly didn't trust them.

I could never predict how girls were going to act. They were often emotional and very competitive. By practicing my avoidance skills, along with a deeply established pattern of people pleasing, I managed to have lots of super-ficial relationships and spent most of my time with boys. As I grew older, I protected myself from other girls, sought value and affirmation from work and men, and generally rejected my own gender's offer of help or friendship.

I am very sad to say that to this day, I do not have one girl-friend relationship intact from those early years of my life.

MY FIRST REAL GIRLFRIEND

My view of women began to change in 1991 when God brought an amazing gift into my life. Her name was Lee Ann.

Ashley was only six months old and Mark and I had just moved to a new community. We were starting a busi-ness from scratch. I was searching for a job. We were not connected to a church. We had only a few friends. It was a rocky season in our marriage. I was in a difficult situation and, truthfully, I was a difficult person.

One afternoon, Lee Ann knocked on my door and wel-comed me to the neighborhood. I don't know how she got past all my prickly edges, but she did.

There was something different about Lee Ann. First of all, she was consistently kind. She never said an ugly word about anyone. In addition, she was innately optimistic. She looked at every situation with a certain expectation of a positive outcome.

She helped me find a babysitter, encouraged me to attend the local block party, invited us over to play cards, and became my best walking buddy. She was also the big-gest prankster I'd ever met. Nothing made her giggle more than a great gag and an opportunity to dress up, be silly, and laugh.

Over the years, Lee Ann loved me. And slowly, sweetly, quietly, she melted my defenses. Before I knew it, I loved her too. She taught me a number of important things—like how to phrase a great question, how to listen well to others, how to endure hardship, how to believe the best of others, and how to present Jesus without religious trappings or heavy condemnation. She showed me how to love my husband more tenderly and how to speak to my daughter with more kindness. She didn't do any of these things with an attitude of instruction. She simply modeled grace, spoke hope, and remained faithful. She mentored me before I even knew what the word meant. She made me glad to be a woman.

I am so glad Lee Ann chose to invest in me right where I was, because that one friendship transformed my life. A longing for authentic, rich, uplifting relationships with women seeped into my bones. I wanted to be for other women what Lee Ann was to me: a good friend who became a catalyst for change and pointed the way to Jesus Christ.

I know for a fact one good girlfriend can cure a lot of woes, just like one good soldier on the battlefield can turn the tide of an engagement.

It wasn't until David stepped up to defy Goliath that the clash between Israel and the Philistines took a turn for the better. Thousands of his countrymen had stood by for several days, listening to the giant taunt them and mock God. With one steady, practiced release of a smooth, round stone from his sling, young David annihilated God's enemy and defeated an entire army.

One good soldier is powerful. So is one good girlfriend.

ONE FRIENDSHIP LEADS TO OTHERS

Ever since Lee Ann came into my life, the way I view women has changed. Everywhere I look, I see another marvelous example of my gender. When I meet her, I recognize her goodness, her potential, her hope, her destiny, and her influence. My heart is quick to embrace her, to value her, to encourage her. I have discovered women are awesome!

Many of those special ladies were in my life all along, but I didn't realize it. When my eyes were opened through love, my perceptions were forever changed.

It seems I'm not alone. Many women have shared with me encouraging stories of how a girlfriend impacted their lives in positive ways. Allow me to share some of them with you:

> Over the years, God sent just the right women at just the right time so we could journey together…some for a season, some for a particular reason, and some for a lifetime.

> God has blessed me with a few loving, loyal friends who are steadfast and stick closer than a brother. I thank God for them daily and wouldn't trade them for anything. I no longer look for quantity in my friendships. Instead I appreciate the quality of these women. We don't have the luxury of spending as much time together as we would like, but the occasions when we do are precious. I am a blessed woman indeed.

Each of my friends has deposited something in me along the way, and for that I am grateful. My hope is that with a healed heart I too can deposit something into the lives of others at just the right time. It makes me smile to know God will entrust those precious women to me to love on and encourage, just as I was once entrusted to someone.

I have been forgiven much, so I've made a conscious decision to forgive those who have hurt me. To truly express my appreciation for all God has forgiven me for, I need to grant grace and mercy to others. I believe making forgiveness a lifestyle can change entire families for generations to come. I take every opportunity to train my kids with what has been given to me. My prayer is to leave a legacy of forgiveness, love, and a close-knit family that grows with each generation.

DAUGHTERS

My parents were very young when I was born and, in some ways, I feel like I came into the world fully grown. In my early years, people often thought I was older than I was. I had the usual traits of a firstborn/only child. I was a natural leader. I could carry on adult conversations with ease. I spent most of my time in the presence of grown-ups. As a teenager, I had no interest in young kids and I was a terrible babysitter. As a young adult, some days I felt downright ancient.

Although I think the consequences of being an only child are mostly positive, there was one outcome I didn't realize until I was much older. I never really grasped what it means to be a daughter.

Obviously I am a daughter, but I find it much more natural to think like a mother than like a daughter.

This shortcoming was magnified when I started having children of my own. Since I expected my kids to "hit the ground running," I tended to put pressure on them to grow up too fast. I encouraged them to hurry past their childhood rather than embracing all the seasons and benefits of youth.

It took many years and some significant trials for me to really believe God saw me as a daughter. It took a long time for me to believe He would make a way for me, defend me, or protect me, give me favor, or just love me—simply because I was His child.

Even now, I still need to be taught how to be a daughter. And God must know that, because He continually sends me "mothers" to teach me about my needs.

I know for a fact one good girlfriend can cure a lot of woes.

I have made many great friendships since Mark and I relocated to the Dallas/Fort Worth metroplex. But there is a small cluster of women from West Texas who knew me when my podium was the kitchen table and "ministry moments" happened with four children at my feet. (That's still my favorite place to have a God conversation!)

These women were a part of my life during a time of

rapid spiritual development. We spent many precious hours God-chasing together. We were passionate, authentic, vulnerable, and as a result God did something unexplainable in our hearts. He gathered us and allowed us to experience all the seasons of a woman's life together. He also used these friends to especially teach me about the joys of being a daughter.

I thank God daily for these beautiful friends. Each one taught me something about how to be a daughter, and I am grateful for their willingness to give me the time to properly grow up. While I walked with them, I grew to be a healthy daughter and began my journey toward becoming a healthy mom. By watching them, I learned more about how a daughter thinks and acts. I realized I needed to repent for an attitude of independence and self-reliance, which often sparked rebellion in me. I started asking God for His favor and for a demonstration of His love. And a place in me that had been shut off for years began to bloom.

Then He dispersed us. Some moved to other cities, even to other states, and one was sent to a different country. We don't see each other often anymore. (Thank goodness for Facebook, Twitter, and blogs!) Yet despite the geographic distance, I know in a moment of need they would stand with me. As a matter of fact, they have already proven so. And I would do the same for them.

Sometimes you are in an abundantly blessed season and don't even realize it until it's gone. My friends and I had no idea our time together would end so soon, that it was so unique, or that it would never come again. This experience made me want to take every opportunity to go deep in my current relationships.

SISTERS

Thanks to the life-changing relationships I enjoyed during my years in West Texas, I arrived in the Dallas/Fort Worth area healthier and more confident of God's unconditional love for me. During my early years at Gateway Church, He allowed me to connect with and be encouraged by several different ladies. He continued to demonstrate how other women could fill in my emotional barrenness.

As I learned how to be a healthy daughter, much to my surprise I discovered another area of my life that was undeveloped. I also had no idea what it meant to be a sister.

This revelation came to me one day while driving down the interstate. My mom was having some significant health issues, and I was feeling overwhelmed by the circumstances and responsibility of such weighty decisions. I felt very alone.

As I drove down the road talking to the Lord about my concerns, I told Him, "I wish I had a sibling to share this with, someone to call and talk it through, someone to help."

He responded, "I have given you three sisters."

I knew the Lord was speaking to me about some very close friends. Over the previous few years, several women had come into my life at a critical moment.

He wants every human being He ever created to be His friend. And that includes you.

When I returned from my road trip, I approached these women and confessed my feelings. I told them I needed some sisters and asked them to help me grow in this area. I learned I could call on them in both good and bad moments. I'm still enjoying discovering sister relationships and how they help me be a part of a family. My sisters have touched a place that was relationally cold and reconnected me to my sense of belonging.

I have also been given the gift of a whole family of "extended relatives." I count it as one of my greatest joys to serve the women of Gateway Church during this season of my life. I have been loved and led to greater wholeness. Over the years, I've been steeped in grace. I've been praised in public and instructed in private. God has allowed my relationships to create a safe place in me for the exposure of my greatest insecurities and weaknesses…and still find acceptance.

Countless other women have critically shaped me in this season. My mother continues to love me into wholeness. My daughter has taught me so much. Extended family members have received me with love and modeled an acceptance and faithfulness that continues to bless me.

I still have a lot of work to do. Yet with each giving of my heart, I have received more than I have given. I have the privilege of fully being a daughter, a sister, and a mother. As a result, I am better, stronger, and never lonely.

WE ARE IN GOOD COMPANY

In military terms a company is defined as a small unit of soldiers. Christ, as our friend, calls us to become part of

His company and positions us to become friends and serve with others. When we build relationships with others in our lives, we are in good company.

The Bible talks a lot about God being friends with people who love Him.

- The Lord spoke to Moses "face to face, as one speaks to a friend" (Exod. 33:11).

- God called Abraham "My friend" (Isa. 41:8, MEV).

- Job said, "When I was in my prime, God's friendship was felt in my home" (Job 29:4).

- Jesus referred to Lazarus as "our friend" (John 11:11, MEV).

- Jesus told His disciples, "You are My friends, since I have told you everything the Father told me" (John 15:15).

Just think of it. You have the same friend as Moses, Abraham, Job, Lazarus, and Jesus's disciples.

Maybe you don't feel like you belong in such lofty company. Well, Jesus was also called "a friend of tax collectors and other sinners" (Matt. 11:19, Luke 7:34). When He was speaking to the multitudes, He called them "dear friends" (Luke 12:4). Jesus referred to "the women who had followed him from Galilee" as friends (Luke 23:49). He even called Judas "my friend" immediately before he betrayed Him (Matt. 26:50).

You see, God isn't picky about whom He'll befriend. He

wants every human being He ever created to be His friend. And that includes you.

It's time to get over your fears and make some new friends. If you don't garner your courage and just begin, you will never know the amazing gift of a good girlfriend.

· · ·

QUESTIONS FOR REFLECTION

This whole conversation about girlfriends makes some of us uncomfortable. I just imagine you might be thinking, "Thanks, but no thanks." I can relate. I definitely started out with that frame of mind. Lots of us would rather walk on by than deal with "drama." This approach is a short-term coping mechanism, and it yields only isolation and loss. As I ask you to think about your own girlfriends, please give yourself and others more grace. Let's work on being hard to offend and easy to approach. Don't forget your journal as we begin.

Who was/is your best girlfriend? What qualities do you love about her? How has she impacted your life?

Have you ever told this girlfriend how she has impacted you? If it's possible, take a little time and send a letter, an e-mail, or a text, letting your friend know how she has positively impacted your life.

Do you find it easier to think like a "mother" or a "daughter"? Why do you think that is?

Write out some positive qualities of a mother and some positive qualities of a daughter. Then compare the two. Describe some ways in which mothers and daughters can positively impact one another.

When I told the Lord I wished I had a sibling to share my burdens with, He responded, "I have given you three sisters."

Read the story in this chapter about how God identified my "sisters." Being a "sister" in this way requires vulnerability. You will need to be open with another woman, perhaps exposing some areas you've never exposed before. I hope you've been receiving healing in some areas so you will reach out to others and discover those precious "sister" relationships for yourself.

Journal your feelings about my experience. Have you ever had an experience like this of your own? If you haven't found your "sisters" yet, ask God to show them to you. It's likely they are already in your life and you just don't know it yet.

Take a moment to identify any other women who may have functioned in your life as a mother, a daughter, or a sister. Then ask yourself if you serve in these roles to others. Is there anyone on this list that you feel especially close to? Explain.

You see, God isn't picky about whom He'll befriend. He wants every human being He ever created to be His friend. And that includes you.

Have you ever considered you could be "friends" with God? What does it feel like to consider the possibility?

Go back and review the "friend" scriptures listed in this chapter. Ask God to show you how He views you as His friend.

CHAPTER ELEVEN

Declaring a Cease-Fire

HEALTHY FEMALE RELATIONSHIPS ARE POSSIBLE AND POWERFUL

• • •

Blessed are the peacemakers, for they
shall be called the sons of God.
Matthew 5:9, MEV

Now that we are aware of the war around us, we can guard our hearts against the enemy's attacks. Those fiery darts Satan tries to use to penetrate your heart can be defensively turned away; you can engage in the right war, and begin to fire right back!

But we need to stop fighting among ourselves. The time has come to call a cease-fire between our sisters and us. Why not dare to go a step further and actually declare peace?

I realize it's a bit naïve to think we could all just hold hands and make up. And I don't want a false kind of peace—the kind that requires many rules and giant consequences. The peace I'm thinking of comes from within and it happens one person at a time. I'm looking toward a culture shift that will allow us to lay down our weapons of war and embrace a lifestyle of love.

To accomplish this, you and I will need to come to the negotiation table and begin again. Each of us must do the work of repentance and forgiveness. We need to make a conscious choice to change the way we think and the way we act. We have to decide to invest in the women around us.

I know I'm talking about something radically counterculture. But it is possible.

A TIME LIKE THIS

One of the most powerful women in the Bible started out as an exile, an orphan, and a peasant girl.

When Hadassah's parents died, her uncle Mordecai took her in. Just as she was coming of age, word came to their village that the king was seeking a new queen.

All of the single girls in the kingdom were to be taken before the king for his consideration. In the end Hadassah was among the young women chosen to do this.

As the troops were taking his niece away, Mordecai whispered in her ear, "Don't tell anyone about your nationality or family background." You see, the king did not treat exiles from Jerusalem very kindly. Fearing for his young niece's life, Mordecai suggested Hadassah use her non-Jewish name, Esther.

The time has come to call a cease-fire between our sisters and us. Why not dare to go a step further and actually declare peace?

Out of all the lovely women being considered to become the new queen, the king chose Esther. She didn't realize it at the time, but God not only knew what was happening to her, but He'd planned this all along. He had a special reason for putting Esther in this situation.

When one of the king's top advisors, who hated the Jews, devised a plan to kill them, Esther was in a unique position to save her people from annihilation. When she hesitated to risk her life by going to the king without a proper invitation, confessing her true nationality and begging for her people's lives, her uncle posed this crucial question to her: "Who knows if perhaps you were made queen for just such a time as this?" (Esther 4:14).

You and I are in a similar predicament today. The "Queen Vashtis" of our prior generations have left a life-threatening situation for us. They've opened doors to an enemy that wants to annihilate our gender and our offspring. Many of us have been left orphaned, abandoned, and in spiritual poverty. Some of us are even using false names and denying our inheritance.

Esther knew her role as queen was a tremendous responsibility. It was also a test. Being in that position presented her with a unique opportunity to save the lives of her people. Would she rise to the task?

Esther summoned her courage and faced the challenge before her. She asked everyone she knew to fast for three days. Then she followed the leading of the Lord in her sticky situation. She eventually made her request known to the king. As a result she saved her own life and the lives of her people. The wicked advisor got his just desserts, her uncle was given a position of authority, and the messianic line was preserved. Esther reigned as queen for many years.

CULTURAL CHANGE IS POSSIBLE

Esther changed her world because of what she believed, what she said, and what she did. Our civilization is created by what we believe, what we say, and what we do. *What you do matters. What you think has value. What you say is powerful.*

Every nation has a culture. So does every organization, family, or gathering. Culture is defined as "the integrated pattern of human knowledge, belief, and behavior that depends on the capacity for learning and transmitting knowledge to succeeding generations."[1] I would propose a slight change in this definition. What if culture was defined as a pattern of divine knowledge, belief, and behavior?

You and I are citizens of a heavenly society. Though we live in a natural world and are subject to the customs around us, there lies within each of us a godly culture. The longer we walk with the Lord and the greater our love for Him, the stronger this heavenly culture shines.

You can change the culture around you too. When we walk in unity with our sisters, the kingdom becomes stronger, more vibrant, more powerful, and more visible. This "kingdom culture" unifies us and gives us the potential to change our world; this kind of change always starts with *one person* and *one idea*.

ONE IDEA CAN CHANGE YOUR WORLD

In the early 1990s my husband and I attended a local church. Through a small group of couples we encountered life-changing teaching and practical application of God's Word mixed with relational accountability. This was the beginning of our spiritual growth.

Mark and I were involved in a discipleship class where we took a spiritual gifts inventory. I laughed out loud when I saw the results, because my number one spiritual gift was "shepherd." As I put it away, I joked with my husband they forgot to ask my gender. In my heart, I was disappointed because I thought the test was going to help me figure out who I was. Since I assumed being female precluded me from becoming a shepherd, I dismissed the test and quietly put it away.

A few years later, Mark and I transitioned to another church, where there was more opportunity to recognize and train individuals who showed a high level of care and concern for the congregation, regardless of gender. As we planted ourselves in that community, my natural bent to gather women and encourage them was allowed to operate. I did not actively pursue becoming identified as a leader. I just served and sowed my heart into the people around me. Before long, I was asked to lead the women's efforts. I offered Bible studies, formed small groups, held an occasional gathering, and even developed a leadership track for women. God had been developing in me a passion to see women healed and whole. He caused me to fall in love with

His precious daughters. My desires were falling in line with His desires.

After walking awhile in this informal leadership role, I began to think I might be a shepherd after all. It seemed my gifts did not require a position or a title to operate. All they needed was a safe place and a pure motive.

I came to realize that if I were never formally recognized as a leader, it would not make a difference. I am created and designed to love people and lead them to Jesus, and so are you.

Within a few weeks of this revelation, I was invited to formally serve as the pastor of women at our church. It was not a significant change on the outside or any big deal to anyone else. I just kept doing what I was already doing: loving people. But this was a significant affirmation in my heart, a special gift from the Father and a sign to me that there is nothing God is asking me to do that He won't equip and release me to do if I will stay the course. He showed me that what was impossible in my mind was possible with Him. Over the years, I've moved in and out of the formal title of pastor. But not once in all these years has my heart drifted from the call.

One idea changed my thinking. And as I disagreed with my natural culture and agreed with God's heavenly culture, my outlook shifted—and so did my life.

RADICAL CHANGE

As you've read about the radical changes that have taken place in my life and my attitudes, perhaps you've been thinking, "That's nice for her, but she doesn't understand my situation." I know that feeling. I've been there.

Not long ago, I was standing at the edge of a huge chasm, looking down into a pit of pain and seeing greener grass on the other side. I wanted my relationships to be different, but I didn't know how to change them. I saw others walking in a wholeness I had not experienced. I wanted what they had, but I didn't believe I could have it.

But Jesus has bridged the gap between our inabilities and God's limitless power. He took me by the hand and led me across the chasm, one step at a time.

What you do matters. What you think has value. What you say is powerful.

Each step of the journey required a giant leap of faith for me. I chose to believe God was good, even when my circumstance and relationships were bad. Once I trusted in His goodness, I began to experience breakthrough. He took me past all my reasoning, fear, and pain to a place where I could receive what I longed for—and what He wanted to give me all along.

You too can cross the chasm of pain and walk into something amazing: God's plan for your life. You just have to take a leap of faith.

DARE TO BE DIFFERENT

I'm not a natural thrill seeker. I avoid roller coasters. I'll never jump out of an airplane, and I don't really like heights. But in the Spirit I am becoming fearless. I have come to enjoy the risks involved in being different. I'm okay with presenting a message that no one else is speaking. I'm willing to go first in a new relationship. I want to change the way women relate to one another, and I'm starting with me.

Risking rejection in an effort to initiate friendships, restore broken relationships, or reach out to strangers is scary and often contrary to what we consider "normal." Romans 12:2 says, "Don't copy the behavior and customs of this world, but let God transform you into a new person by changing the way you think. Then you will learn to know God's will for you, which is good and pleasing and perfect."

Jesus was a fearless revolutionary. He experienced some awkward moments as He dared to reach out to others. He shook up the religious community and boldly embraced confrontation. He preferred to hang out with sinners, and apparently He loved a good party. He'd go out of His way to meet a stranger, even one whom society said He shouldn't go near. He touched lepers, healed the sick, and called into service a circle of people who, according to the standard of the day, were unqualified for ministry. He gave His life out of love for His brothers and sisters.

This "kingdom culture" unifies us and gives us the potential to change our world; this kind of change always starts with *one person* and *one idea*.

He was especially revolutionary in His approach to women. He valued them, and He demonstrated a different way of responding to them. He had women on the road with Him. Women paid for His ministry. They were the fund-raisers and the distributors to the needy. Women were teachers and servants. They even came and sat at His feet as he taught. (All this was pretty edgy for the day.) When He was on the cross, the person He worried most about was a woman, His mother. And the first person He told He had risen from the dead was a woman.

Jesus's approval, love, and empowerment of women prove He has an especially tender place in His heart for us. We should challenge one another to follow in His footsteps, to become counter-culture in our relationships. If He placed such a high value on women, we should too.

BUILD A BRIDGE

Bridges provide safe passage over a gap or barrier. They create connections that did not exist before and open up new territory for acquisition and exploration. Relationships are bridges that connect people, even if they are far apart— geographically, mentally, emotionally, or even spiritually.

The privilege of constructing relational bridges among our gender rests on us. If we truly want our daughters and ourselves to be whole, strong, powerful, and full of love, you and I must do the hard work required to establish a different approach, a different response, and a different answer. We must build bridges.

I once had a vision of walking with a group of women who fully represented every gift and fruit of the Holy Spirit.

Among us were apostles, evangelists, prophets, pastors, and teachers. There were those who were strong in the gifts of hospitality, mercy, leadership, administration, healing, and miracles. I was among a throng of ladies who were joyfully using their gifts to bless others. There was no competition or comparison. Each gift was valued equally. And the fruit of this body was more and more women entered the circle and brought their gifts to the table.

> **I want to change the way women relate to one another, and I'm starting with me.**

I have held this vision close to my heart for years and often pray to see it in the natural before the end of my life. Occasionally I catch a glimpse of this dynamic, and when I see it my spirit leaps.

A BLESSING BOX

Within two weeks of being diagnosed with breast cancer, I was scheduled for chemotherapy. The night before I went in for my first treatment, some precious women showed up at my house with a gift: a beautiful, ornate box they called a blessing box. Several people who loved me had prepared a variety of special surprises and encouraging notes, which they'd placed in this box. The women who gave me the gift asked me to wait until I was in the chemo room to open it.

The next morning, accompanied by a dear friend and clutching my blessing box, I trembled as my doctor led me to the chemo room. This was a frightening place, where death seemed to lurk in every corner. I didn't know what to expect. To be honest, I was more afraid of what I would find in the chair beside me than what was about to drip into my veins. What if people were unkind? What if they shared things that might frighten me? What if how sick they were compromised my own faith in healing? I wasn't sure I was strong enough to get through this experience.

I sat down and the nurse hooked me up. When I was settled, my friend suggested I open the blessing box. With shaking fingers, I removed the lid. Inside I found bracelets, lip gloss, passages of Scripture written on pretty paper, prophetic words, worship music—all kinds of things which spoke life to me. Many women, with much love, had drawn together and contributed what they could to encourage me and give me hope. Looking through the items, I laughed. I wept.

Peace means much more than simply the absence of war and conflict. The Hebrew word for peace— *shalom*—signifies both prosperity and tranquility.

I soon realized my friend and I had the attention of other people in the room. Everyone around me seemed to need the same encouragement I did. So we started passing the blessing box around and sharing it with the other patients. As my blessing box traveled across the room, others laughed and talked. The atmosphere of death and depression lifted as people shared in this special gift. My friends who'd intended to bless me had initiated an overflow of love and joy.

Those same faithful friends prepared more blessing boxes for my second and third rounds of chemotherapy. Some of the notes of encouragement came from women I didn't know. People took time to do something special for me even though I had never done anything like that for them.

My friends reminded me of the spiritual principle of reaping and sowing. For years I have been a sower of encouragement in the lives of many women. It has been my joy to invest in a multitude of friends. I have planted many seeds in the lives of others. And in the moment of my need, the bread I'd cast upon the waters came back to me a hundredfold. (See Ecclesiastes 11:1, KJV.) I had a harvest of relationships, love, and support.

If we pull together, sow together, and reap together, we will set in motion a movement of love, acceptance, and peace that will change the generations that follow us.

The ministry of those blessing boxes multiplied. Others caught the vision and started putting together blessing boxes to encourage more people. What was meant to bless one individual multiplied and produced a harvest large enough to feed many.

Many women prayed for me, surrounded me, and carried me in the early days of my cancer treatments. I believe those who interceded for me helped save my life. My community, my family, my sisters all stood in the gap and ministered to me. It was like catching a glimpse of that vision again. I experienced a group of women with every gift and fruit of the Holy Spirit, joyfully using their gifts to bless me.

Do not underestimate the power of encouragement, love, and life-giving. The simplest things say, "I love you. I care." And you never know when you will be in a position to receive what you have sown.

DECLARE PEACE

In the movie *Miss Congeniality* Gracie Hart is asked, "What is the one most important thing our society needs?" She answers, "That would be harsher punishment for parole violators." After a long pause, she adds, "And world peace!"[2]

The crowd cheers ecstatically. After all, everyone wants world peace. But how do we achieve it? Only one person can bring us peace: Jesus Christ. He is called the Prince of Peace. Peace means much more than simply the absence of war and conflict. The Hebrew word for peace—*shalom*—signifies both prosperity and tranquility. Jesus is the bringer of true peace. Peace is His nature. It is His passion. He said, "Peace I leave with you. My peace I give to you" (John 14:27, MEV). Once we belong to Him, you and I can experience a foretaste of what true world peace will one day be like.

God is calling us to rise above our personal agendas, fears, and wounds, and draw near to one another in a way that synergizes our individual callings. Those of us who have been walking longer should lead the way. If we pull together, sow together, and reap together, we will set in motion a revolution of love and peace which will change the generations that follow us. Our daughters and grand-daughters will walk strong and whole, free of our past, empowered to bring hope and healing to others. Just imagine what it would look and feel like to declare a cease-fire on toxic female relationships.

· · ·

QUESTIONS FOR REFLECTION

In this section I've been casting vision for a love revolution and encouraging you to declare a cease-fire among our toxic relationships. Do you believe a revolution is even possible? What would it take for you to believe? What would it take for you to begin? This is a great time in our journey to set some direction for your future. Take a few moments to develop some action steps—some goals—that will help you move forward differently. Think about the relationships closest to you first. Ask God for wisdom and fresh ideas, and then record in your journal your plan of action.

Describe how the culture around you values women. Then consider how our heavenly culture values women. What differences or similarities do you see?

Take some time to thumb through the Gospels of Matthew, Mark, Luke, and John. Consider them with a fresh eye toward Jesus's treatment of women. Journal what you find.

Consider the question posed to Hadassah (Esther): "Yet who knows whether you have come to the kingdom for such a time as this?" (Esther 4:14, NKJV). You are just like Esther, with your own unique gifts, calling, and influence. God has placed you here and now with purpose.

How does that make you feel? Are there any specific responsibilities you feel called to address? Journal your thoughts.

What would it look like for you to operate in a way that was contrary to your culture in regards to your female relationships? How would it change your life?

We've discussed many ways in which we as women can counteract the culture around us, simply by restoring and investing in relationships with other women. Romans 12:2 says, "Don't copy the behavior and customs of this world, but let God transform you into a new person by changing the way you think. Then you will learn to know God's will for you, which is good and pleasing and perfect."

Has your thinking about women changed?

Has your thinking about relationships changed? Please explain.

Have you noticed any new patterns of thought about mothers, sisters, or friends? How will you respond to these new ways of thinking? Journal your thoughts.

Determine today to resist comparing yourself to others but rather embrace yourself fully. Allow the other women around you to be themselves as well. Practice noticing and appreciating what is unique about everyone.

What are some things that make you unique? What is it about you that stands out and speaks of God's design? Why do you suppose God crafted each person so uniquely?

Is there someone in your life who could use some encouragement? Spend some time creating your own "Blessing Box" experience. Maybe you could share a meal (I always say in moments of pain or joy, food always says I love you), send a note of encouragement, or pray for that person, and watch how God uses it to bless others.

CHAPTER TWELVE

No One Left Behind

Bringing Peace to Yourself— And Your Girlfriends Too

. . .

God didn't set us up for an angry rejection but for salvation by our Master, Jesus Christ. He died for us, a death that triggered life. Whether we're awake with the living or asleep with the dead, we're alive with him! So speak encouraging words to one another. Build up hope so you'll all be together in this, no one left out, no one left behind. I know you're already doing this; just keep on doing it.
1 Thessalonians 5:9–11, THE MESSAGE

In the midst of an intense battle it is easy to get separated from your troop. When the fight is raging, bombs are exploding, and smoke cascades, it's difficult to hear, see, or gauge your position. Isolation is dangerous. The threat of death is dramatically amplified when you are injured or alone.

This is why the military has a code of conduct called "no one left behind." There is a brotherhood on the battlefield that says, "I won't leave you to die alone or be captured by the enemy. You and I are in this together. We are getting out of here together." This is the type of heroic attitude that leads to Purple Hearts and stories of bravery.

Some of our sisters are disoriented in the midst of this war for our womanhood. They are having difficulty hearing the truth or seeing the actions of other females as friendly. They are stumbling about like walking wounded, trying to find their home base. Many have been injured and left on the battlefield.

Will those of us who are more battle savvy, better armed, or just more fortunate leave them behind? Or will we risk our own comfort to rescue them and bring them back into the ranks where their wounds will be healed so they can reenter the battle healthy and whole?

FRESH STARTS

I love fresh starts, don't you? There's something awesome about the opportunity to clear the decks and begin again. I enjoy opening the cover of a brand-new book or the potential of a blank piece of paper. How about a set of just-washed sheets on your bed, or getting a mulligan when you whiff the ball? There's something about a new start that gives us a sense of hope and a fresh wind in our sails.

Isn't that the reason we make New Year's resolutions or set goals? We take a look at where we've been and where we thought we'd be by now. We evaluate our progress, celebrate our breakthroughs, deal with our disappointments, and consider a new plan of action. That's why the changing of the calendar from December to January fills me with a sense of hope.

When I received the heart-stopping diagnosis of breast cancer, the initial trauma left me shell-shocked, openly exposed on a battlefield for my health. Thankfully, some experienced soldiers in this fight came to my rescue. They took my hand and led me to safety and hope. Thanks to them I learned this diagnosis was not the end, but a fresh start for me.

Maybe you've had a few "oh no" moments too. This battle called life may have left you standing on the sidelines. You might have sustained a few hateful blows from our enemy, or maybe even some friendly fire from those you love. Well, be encouraged! Our God is all about the second chance. He's always inviting us to begin again with Him. He never leaves us on the battlefield alone or unequipped. There are countless sisters in the same territory who want to rush to your aid. In the very place you thought you were beyond recovery, you can, in fact, be saved.

ENJOY THE JOURNEY

A few months after my diagnosis a coworker said to me, "Take time to enjoy the journey."

I took that advice to heart. The journey hasn't all been pleasant, of course. But every day I have encountered a faithful God who is kinder than I thought, wiser than I knew, and more compassionate than I ever imagined. I've been given a second chance, a fresh start, a do-over. What seemed to be the worst thing that could possibly happen to me has actually brought tremendous blessing.

I am experiencing renewal in my body, soul, and spirit. Although we can't undo the past, we can begin again. This is the essence of the salvation experience—the rebirth. When we accept Christ as Savior, we begin again. When we forgive, we begin again. When we love one another, we begin again.

You can begin again too. God can take your response to His invitation and begin to renew every area of your life.

- *God can renew your spirit.* Psalm 51:10 says, "Create in me a pure heart, O God, and renew a steadfast spirit within me" (NIV).

- *God can renew your mind.* Romans 12:2 says, "Do not conform to the pattern of this world, but be transformed by the renewing of your mind" (NIV).

- *God can renew your past.* Isaiah 61:4 says, "They will rebuild the ancient ruins and restore the places long devastated; they will renew the ruined cities that have been devastated for generations" (NIV).

- *God can renew your strength.* Isaiah 40:31 says, "Those who hope in the Lord will renew their strength" (NIV).

- *God can renew your body.* Second Corinthians 4:16 says, "Do not lose heart. Though outwardly we are wasting away, yet inwardly we are being renewed day by day" (NIV).

So how do you get started on the road to renewal? Here are a few of my best tips.

GET OUT OF YOUR COMFORT ZONE

You will not be able to truly overcome your past pain until you dare to begin again. In order to grow strong, you have to take back what has been stolen from you. You have to begin cultivating something different in the place of your wounding.

When we've been hurt, it's a natural tendency of self-preservation to stay away from anyone who might cause us more pain. As a result we sometimes forfeit the very relationships that could help us grow strong and whole.

Our God is all about the second chance.

If you're ready to make some real friends, you're going to have to change your mind about your methods of relating to women and take a risk. You'll need to step out into some scary territory. Yes, you could get hurt. You might be rejected. Someone may touch an old wound. You'll probably feel uncomfortable, but the results will be well worth the cost.

Once you make up your mind that you are going to change your old patterns of thinking and acting, you'll be ready for the second major step toward a new life.

SHOW UP

In Paul's letter to the Romans, he tells them, "One of the things I always pray for is the opportunity, God willing, to come at last to see you. For I long to visit you so I can bring you some spiritual gift that will help you grow strong in the Lord. When we get together, I want to encourage you in your faith, but I also want to be encouraged by yours" (Rom. 1:10–12).

This verse reminds me of why it is so important for us to draw together. When we are able to share with another, we can both give and receive wonderful encouragement.

When you're ready to start forging new relationships, choose your potential friends wisely. We usually select friends and spouses who are of equal emotional maturity and health. We also tend to become like the people we spend time with. If you hang around women who are healthy, you will become healthy too. If they are kind, you will learn to be kind. Whatever is in others will get into you. And what's in you can be imparted to them.

Consider joining any shared experience that stirs your passion: church, PTA, biking club, a fitness center. Seek a place that has values and purpose members can be unified about. Potential friends are everywhere!

REACH OUT

If you put out a vibe that indicates you're looking to make friends, you might be surprised at how many women respond. As the saying goes, if you want to have a friend you need to be a friend. Don't wait for others to approach you. Take a risk and reach out to another.

You and I will never be able to establish new friendships if we don't risk initial rejection.

I used to be shy with women I didn't know, but now I like to be bold. At some point you will have to risk an experience with a woman wounder. The only bonds that hold us are the ones we have yet to remove.

If I see someone new, I'll just stick out my hand and say, "Hi, my name is Jan." If I wait a moment, she'll usually tell me her name. Then I ask a simple question about her, like, "How are you today?" I just take a moment and try to connect in some small and unthreatening way.

This simple act still requires courage on my part. After all she might not want to speak to me. She might be too busy for me or think I'm strange. It might be awkward.

At some point, you will have to risk an experience with a woman wounder.

But what if she does want to get to know me? What if she's just like me, longing to make a new friend, willing to connect? What if she too is feeling awkward or lonely or wondering how to get to know someone? You and I will never be able to establish new friendships if we don't risk initial rejection.

Even if a new relationship is a little shaky at the beginning, it doesn't mean you should run away. You have to exercise grace for those uncomfortable initial moments.

The first time Lee Ann came to my door, I'm sure I was a little weird. I didn't know how to be hospitable to this friendly neighbor who wanted to know me.

GET THE BALL ROLLING...
AND KEEP IT GOING

Once you've experienced one or more healthy female relationships, you can become a mentor to someone else. You can be a "mother to mothers." As your natural tendency to nurture is set free, you will have everything you need to be healed and to help others heal.

Jesus said a good shepherd will leave the many to go find one lost sheep and bring it back into the fold (Luke 15:3–6). He did that for you and for me, to bring us salvation. And He wants us to follow His example.

There's safety and relationship in community. Isolation is dangerous, particularly for a woman. The enemy wants us to separate from our sisters so he can attack us. So be alert. Don't wander off by yourself.

In addition, pay attention to the women on the outer edges of your social circle. If you notice someone slipping away, take action. Invite her out for coffee or lunch. Send her a note of encouragement. Pray for her. Don't force her to open up to you. Just be a friend. Show that you care. Share your heart and your life with her, and be a safe place for her to share too.

I WON'T LEAVE YOU BEHIND

I love my children with all my heart, yet I know I have wounded them. I am determined not to let them stay in those wounds. I have to seek their forgiveness and repair our relationships so we can go on together. They are my offspring, and I am their primary protection against an enemy who hates them. I will not leave them behind in pursuit of my own mission and passion. If you and I gain the whole world but lose our children, we've lost everything.

In addition to my biological children I am involved in the lives of many amazing women. Sadly some of them are walking wounded, casualties of this war on our gender. I have decided I will not go on without them either.

I can't bear the thought that I would walk through my life and not take the time to say to every woman within my reach, "Yes, you can! You can declare a cease-fire. You can love women. You can heal your relationships. You can overcome your pain. You can lead others to grace. You can embrace yourself, your daughters, and your girlfriends too. You can love extravagantly."

But I can't reach every woman in the world. That's where you come in!

If you and I gain the whole world but lose our children, we've lost everything.

There are countless women in your life that could be healed if you shared this message with them. You can minister to your daughter, your mother, and your friends. If each of us accepts personal responsibility for our sisters, we can take back our God-given, life-giving name of woman. We will establish a healthy, powerful community of grace.

Together, we have tremendous potential. An entire society of healed, whole, unified women will be a major force for good in the earth.

So tell someone else about what you've learned and what God is doing in and through you. Reach out to your mother, daughters, sisters, and friends. Dare to do something different. Pull back the curtain of your fear and invite others to join you in a cease-fire decision that can begin a revolution of peace. Whether you are in the eye-opening stage of revelation, seeing the damage of wounded women all around you, or moving forward to enter healing, someone needs you. Let's leave no one behind.

THE BATTLE CONTINUES

Have you ever thought about how remarkable it is you are living during this moment in history? When I consider the timing of my birth, I am amazed. I'm not so taken back by the month or day, but by the sheer blessing of having been born during this particular time. I would never have made it in the Dark Ages. The thought of pioneering across the United States makes me tired, and I love indoor plumbing, air-conditioning, and take-out food. I'm custom-made for the twenty-first century!

I'm also grateful for the privilege of being a woman during this era and in this country. We've witnessed the millennium change, the launch of the Internet, and the most massive spread of the gospel ever known. Today women are free to run not only our homes but also businesses and even governments. We live in the wealthiest and most influential nation in the world. We have opportunities, responsibilities, and choices our mothers and grandmothers never dreamed of. *And we know Jesus!*

Not everyone enjoys this privileged position. Women and children around the world live in desperate and difficult times. Some are more than emotionally wounded. They are trapped in poverty, cultural discrimination, even slavery. Oppression comes in many forms: abuse, addiction, depression, hopelessness, hunger, and injustice to name a few. And this is not just in faraway lands and unseen places. Lots of our sisters live in oppressive situations right in our own backyard. *And many do not know Jesus.*

Surely our privilege does not come without a price. Luke 12:48 says, "Great gifts mean great responsibilities; greater gifts, greater responsibilities" (THE MESSAGE).

You and I are poised with both great gifts and great responsibilities. When someone or something is poised, there is a sense of suspended tension. It's in the split second before a lion pounces, before a trigger is pulled, or before an opening curtain is swept back. Everything is prepared, ready, on the brink.

The greatest gift my battle with cancer has given me is the realization my life and my days matter.

There is a change happening among women today. As we walk in peace with one another, we become a force to be reckoned with. Our power is released, God's kingdom dramatically expands, and our enemy is vanquished. There is a shift in the spirit, a swelling up of something big and important, life-changing and lovely.

The war over our gender is not over yet.

There are still battles to be fought, and we have a responsibility to reach out to the women around us who are trapped in lies and wounds and establish love and peace as the foundation of our culture. Even though our enemy continues to stir up war between us in an attempt to leave us powerless and lifeless, we cannot, nor would we want to, negotiate a peace treaty with Satan. Since he is already defeated, the war is won. In the end you and I will win. Through Christ we will crush his head.

> **When we are at peace with one another we become a force to be reckoned with.**

My personal war with cancer isn't over either. But I'm throwing the enemy a few surprise attacks. I'm encouraging fellow survivors. I'm urging women to prioritize self-care and practice preventative measures that can reduce their risk of cancer. I'm making others aware of the importance of early detection as a life-saving measure.

In early 2011 I received an opportunity to expand the impact of my story. I partnered with the National Breast Cancer Foundation (NBCF), whose mission is to save lives by increasing awareness of breast cancer through education and by providing mammograms for those in need. As part of an NBCF project called "Beyond the Shock," I was featured in a documentary in which I share my insights and perspectives as a cancer survivor. I hope my story will inspire courage, hope, and faith in others who are battling illnesses. (If you'd like to view this documentary, visit www .beyondtheshock.com. It is an excellent and encouraging resource for those who've been recently diagnosed and their families.)

Recently I underwent my annual mammograms, ultrasounds, CTs, and PET scans. I had a major scare—something didn't look quite right on one of the tests. I called on my mentors, mothers, sisters, and friends to fight with me again through their prayers and encouragements.

To my relief, I received the "all clear" again. I came out of that fight with a few bruises, but more committed to fighting for my health than ever before.

The incident reminded me afresh of the urgency of numbering my days, valuing my relationships, and considering my legacy.

A LEGACY OF LOVE

The greatest gift my battle with cancer has given me is the realization my life and my days matter. It's not enough to have faith, for "faith without works is dead" (James 2:26, MEV). We must both believe and do.

The name *mother* can't be demanded; it has to be earned through a relationship built with love, care, and tenderness. The relatively impersonal venue of reading words on a page may not be sufficient to establish that kind of relationship between you and me. But even if I've never met you, I sincerely care about you, and I want to deposit something in your life that truly makes a difference for you.

This is why I am passionate about exposing the lies women have believed since Genesis 3 about their true purpose, value, and impact. I want to wake us up to our real enemy, revealing the real war at hand. I am using every weapon I have to demolish the strongholds of our culture and expose the lies of the enemy. I'm rushing to the battlefield to help those who are lost or wounded. I want to minister to them the truth of who they are in Christ. I desire to create in them a different expectation of other women. I'm determined to leave a legacy of love.

All good moms want their children to be more successful, more fruitful than they were. That's my goal for you. I long to see you step up and step into the very things which our enemy has tried to rip from your hands. My desire is for you to suffer less and love more.

Our battle is for our femininity, our culture, our inheritance, and the generations to come. Life and death are in the balance.

In large part you will determine the effectiveness of my legacy. If I have been able to offer a nudge, a tip, a little motherly encouragement or practical advice, if I have put some helpful values into your life, if I have exposed some lies and revealed some truths, then wherever you go and whatever you do there will be a little bit of me in you.

CAN YOU IMAGINE?

Our battle is for our femininity, our culture, our inheritance, and the generations to come. Life and death are in the balance. Our pain can result in either poison or healing. Our past experiences and patterns can be a crucible for something hurtful or they can produce love, passion, and the gift of life for generations to come.

I urge you to carefully evaluate the ideas I've presented here. Look beyond the popular music, reality TV shows, and the daily news and trace your current viewpoints and experiences back to their original source. Wake up to your generational patterns, wounds, and personal pain to allow God to heal them. Better yet, give yourself a little healthy food for thought—some truth. The Word of God is the most life-changing, thought-provoking, culture-shifting idea of this—or any—generation!

Imagine what would happen if we began a revolution of love, respect, mutual celebration, and investment among women.

When we gather—whether two, or twenty, or two thousand—there's potential for change. What we can do alone is much less than what we can do together. We have the potential to shift our culture, change our experience, and rescue our daughters.

It all begins with you and me.

Your legacy can be a fruitful life that will bless many generations to come.

So be at peace. Be powerful. Multiply. Expand. Change

the world around you. Be a life-giving woman, a mother to mothers.

. . .

QUESTIONS FOR REFLECTION

As you begin these final moments of reflection, let me say thank you. Thank you for trusting me with your heart and for allowing your own life to be open before God. As you pull up to my kitchen table one last time, I invite you to review your journal for a few moments and to give thanks for the revelation you've received. If you're still struggling with some of the wounds from your past, feel free to go back to the chapters that impacted you the most. Spend some time with another kind woman processing those things, allowing God to continue to speak His truth to all the wounded and hurting places. Maybe you can even thank Him for the pain or the difficulties. It's not that we want pain, but pain often becomes the catalyst for change. You have something significant to overcome and share. I'm praying as you ponder these final questions you will feel the victory and go forth in confidence.

You have the opportunity to start over in some areas. Make a list of some fresh starts that you need.

How does looking at that list make you feel? Excited? Anxious? What would it look like if God renewed your mind? Your strength? Your spirit? Take your list to God and let Him speak to you about your blank pages.

Then journal your thoughts about each one of those areas.

All real change begins with making a serious decision to do something different.

Are you ready to see real change in your life? In the lives of the women around you?

What will you do differently? How will you step out of your comfort zone in order to see the change you desire?

Make a list of existing friendships where you can invest in change. What action steps can you take right away?

There is a change happening among women today. As we walk in peace with one another, we become a force to be reckoned with. Our power is released, God's kingdom dramatically expands, and our enemy is vanquished. There is a shift in the spirit, a swelling up of something big and important, life-changing and lovely.

Ask God to speak the truth of this statement to your heart. Journal what you hear. Then declare it!

As a final action step, take some time and journal the legacy of love you want to leave for future generations.

Conclusion

The ministry of Gateway Women is a place where every woman can connect, train, and be empowered to impact her world. We are building healthy ministry for women through a team driven focus that is grace filled and empowering. We strive to honor one another, disciple those in our care, and empower every woman to influence her world for the glory of God.

We believe that God created us to be in relationship with Him and with others. Each week, many women in the Dallas/Fort Worth area come together in a variety of settings and find a place to build intimacy, friendship, and accountability.

Under the direction of Debbie Morris, executive pastor of Gateway Women, we have a number of engaging, relevant, and inspiring opportunities for women. We are devoted to creating safe, friendly, and easily accessible environments where women can discuss the realities of life, encourage one another, and engage in a lifestyle of authentic community and spiritual growth. For the latest updates, please visit the website at www.women.gateway people.com.

This ministry is an exciting example of the incredible power Christian women have when we come together to worship our Creator, invest in one another's lives, and share God's love with others. If you're in the Dallas/Fort Worth area I invite you to come visit us. If not I encourage you to find a local Bible-based church where you can enjoy this kind of beautiful fellowship. God is graciously moving among women everywhere, and you are needed right in your own community.

Notes

CHAPTER FIVE
MISSING IN ACTION

1. Gary D. Chapman, *The 5 Love Languages: The Secret to Love That Lasts* (Chicago, IL: Northfield Publishing, 2009).

CHAPTER ELEVEN
DECLARING A CEASE-FIRE

1. *Merriam-Webster's Collegiate Dictionary*, 11th ed. (Springfield, MA: Merriam-Webster, 2003), s.v. "culture."

2. *Miss Congeniality* directed by Donald Petrie (Burbank, CA: Castle Rock Entertainment, 2000).